the Internet

Mac Bride

TEACH YOURSELF BOOKS

Long-renowned as the authoritative source for self-guided learning – with more than 30 million copies sold worldwide – the *Teach Yourself* series includes over 200 titles in the fields of languages, crafts, hobbies, sports, and other leisure activities.

British Library Cataloguing in Publication Data
A catalogue for this title is available from the British Library

Library of Congress Catalog Card Number: 95-68145

First published in UK 1995 by Hodder Headline Plc, 338 Euston Road, London NW1 3BH

First published in US 1995 by NTC Publishing Group, 4255 West Touhy Avenue, Lincolnwood (Chicago), Illinois 60646 – 1975 U.S.A.

Typeset by Mac Bride, Southampton, Hampshire.
Printed in Great Britain by Cox & Wyman Ltd, Reading, Berkshire.

First published 1995
Impression number   10   9   8   7   6   5   4 .
Year   1999   1998   1997   1996

CONTENTS

ACKNOWLEDGEMENTS

This book could not have been written without the help and active support of:

Alan Jay of the PC Users Club;
Susan Mark of CompuServe;
Geoff Lynch of Aladdin's Sonet;
uncounted contributors to the Internet's newsgroups and World Wide Web pages.

The best bits of this book I owe to them; the mistakes are all my own work.

My thanks to you all.

macbride@macdesign.win-uk.net

README

At first sight, the Internet can be a baffling place. It is huge, encompassing many millions of computers and people. During its brief lifetime, its users have devised a number of different ways and hundred of software tools for working on it – with new techniques and programs appearing all the time. They have also evolved a language rich in technicalities and jargon, that may simplify communication between experienced users, but can be a barrier to the novice.

But look closer, and take heart. In reality, the concepts are not hard to understand, and much of the software – especially the most recent – is very simple to use. This book explains the basic concepts of data communications, covers the essentials of setting up a connection to the Internet, outlines many of the facilities available and explores the major tools. Some of the jargon and technical details are unavoidable, but I have kept them to the minimum.

As there are so many different services, software packages and ways of working, and as you will have your own interests, I have not tried to take a straight-line approach to this book. Instead, I have built hot links into the text. When you see a word or phrase **underlined and in bold**, with a reference after it, jump to that section to find out more about the item. And if, when you get into the **World Wide Web**, (2.6), you find that it reminds you of **hypertext** (8.2), that's because it is supposed to!

macbride@macdesign.win-uk.net

April 1995

1

INTO THE INTERNET

1.1 Aims of this chapter

This chapter aims to answer some of the frequently asked questions about the Internet.

- What is the Internet?
- What can I do with it?
- How do I get into it?
- How hard is it to use?
- What hardware and software do I need?
- What will it cost me?

1.2 What is the Internet?

The Internet is an open world-wide communications network, linking together countless thousands of computer networks, through a mixture of private and public telephone lines. Its component networks are individually run by government agencies, universities, and commercial and voluntary organisations. No single organisation owns or controls the Internet, though there is an Internet Society that co-ordinates and sets standards for its use.

The Internet grew out of a long-distance network developed by the US Government's Advanced Research Projects Agency (ARPAnet) in the late 60s. The fast, high-volume telephone links proved reliable and the network was extended over the next 10 years to connect 200 computers in military and research establishments throughout the US and overseas. It demonstrated clearly that internetworking was both practical and highly useful. Some US universities followed by setting up systems of their own. In the mid 80s these joined with the research part of ARPAnet to form the Internet. The important thing to note here is that the Internet was not set up as a commercial venture. There are still *Appropriate Use* rules that restrict the use of the Internet for profit.

Today, most of the world's universities are linked directly or indirectly; many businesses have joined, some to take advantage of the cheap and efficient international communications, some to advertise their wares, and/or provide services, and others to gain access to the mass of on-line data; a significant and growing number of political parties, pressure groups and charities are using it to network their members and get their messages across. These organisations bring many millions of people onto the Internet, but there are also millions of individuals who link in their home computers through one or other of the many service providers. In the UK alone, there are over 100,000 hosts computers on the Internet. As for individuals, CompuServe, the largest service provider, claims a UK membership of 60,000, with 1,000 new users joining each month.

In early Spring 1995, there are over 4.8 million host computers supplying services and information over the Net, and the number of users is estimated to be anything from 20 to 50 million. By the time you read this, those figures will be out of date, for the rate of growth is phenomenal. The number of host computers has doubled every year for the last four years, and there is plenty of scope for future expansion.

—— **1.3 How do I get into it?** ——

People get access to the Internet in one of two ways. Students and staff at colleges and universities, and members of businesses or other organisations that have linked their networks into the Net, will have access through their local network. If you are in this position, and have not been granted it automatically, ask your system administrator for access. (How much access you get and what facilities you can use, will depend on your organisation.)

People who are not part of a linked institution can get access by joining **CompuServe** (7.7, 8.11, 9.8, 10.5), the **PC Users Group** (7.8, 9.6) or one of the other **service providers** (14.1). It is important to realise that most of these offer a range of services to members in addition to access to the Internet. Some of these services are very similar to – but distinct from – those that are available over the Internet; others are unique to the service provider.

The larger providers have nodes (connection points) in many of the major cities, and it is only necessary to dial-in to one of these to get on-line to the world.

To link up this way, you must be able to set up a terminal at home. For this you will need:

● **a computer** – any type will do, though it is easiest to work from a PC running Windows, or from an Apple Macintosh, as there is plenty of software for these.
● **a modem** (Section 4) – to link the computer to the phone lines.
● **a phone socket** within reach of your computer.

● **communications software** (5.2) to manage your connection with distant computers. You may have some simple software already, and this is enough to get you started.

All the other tools you need for further work on the Internet can be obtained through the Internet.

WINDOWS 95 USERS

At the time of writing, Windows 95 was on the horizon, and it may be that you have it now. If you have, then you have a limited access to the Internet through the Microsoft Network. All you will need to do to get on-line, is install a modem and register with the Network.

——— 1.4 What can I do with it? ———

When you have access to the Internet you can:

● **send messages to friends**, academic and business colleagues – and complete strangers – anywhere in the world. The mail will take anything from half an hour to, at the very most, half a day, to get through, and it can cost no more than the price of a few seconds connection time to the service provider.
● **take part in group discussions**, either on CB-style chat lines (except that you type, not talk).
● **pursue a special interest**, hobby or obsession, through one of the thousands of newsgroups, where people from around the world exchange ideas, advice and files.
● **download files** or text, graphics or programs from public data libraries stored on host computers in academic and commercial institutions, or maintained by an interest group.

- **look up information** in an increasing number of reference 'books', such as *Webster's Dictionary*, *Encyclopaedia Britannica* and *The CIA World Factbooks*.
- **perform key word searches on electronic libraries** to find papers that contain references to your chosen topic – and one search scans the linked world!
- **watch video clips**, view exhibitions in art galleries and museums, and look through cameras thousands of miles away.
- **get the latest national and international news**, weather reports, stock market prices and financial advice, travel information – and book your seat! You can even go shopping.
- **join in multi-player games,** contribute to interactive art and graffitti sessions.

... and much, much more. Every day someone somewhere adds something new to the internet.

Which activities you can do depends upon the type of access offered by your service provider.

- A dial-up UUCP (Unix to Unix Copy) conection will let you exchange messages and transfer files, but will not give you the ability to work on remote computers, or to explore **Gopherspace** (2.5) or the **World Wide Web** (2.6).
- For full interactive access to the Internet, with the ability to roam where you will and make use of all the available tools and facilities, you need a **SLIP connection** (6.2).

Not all providers can offer this at present, though they all seem to be moving towards it as fast as they can.

—— 1.5 How hard is it to use? ——

The short answer is, it depends on how you are trying to use it and what you are trying to use it for. There are half a dozen major areas of activity (and other less common ones) on the

Internet, many different software tools that you can use for those activities, a number of underlying concepts and a lot of jargon to describe it all.

If you have a working grasp of the concepts and the jargon, and have the right tools, most things are easy enough to do at an elementary level, and it doesn't take long to learn how to make fuller use of them. Browsing the **World Wide Web** (2.6) with **Netscape** (6.7), or sending and receiving **e-mail** (2.2), for example, require skills and knowledge that can be picked up in half an hour or so – to work at a basic level – and your expertise will grow naturally out of using them.

There are some areas that present more problems than others. The Internet's core is still the academic community and most university systems are built around mainframe computers that run on the Unix operating system. It is only in the last few years that Macintoshes and PCs have been linking into the Internet, and the vast majority of services are provided on Unix machines.

Much of the time, the overlying software makes this invisible, but those activities that run close to the academic/Unix base tend to be less than user-friendly. The academics themselves are friendly, but Unix is not. You should not, for example, try running commands and programs on a distant computer with **telnet** (2.7) without first learning something about Unix.

——— 1.6 What will it cost me? ———

If you are setting up a terminal at home and do not already have a computer, your best bet is probably to buy a PC capable of running Windows – at the very least a 486SX with 4Megabytes of RAM memory, a 150 Megabyte (or larger) hard drive and a colour monitor. At the time of writing, you can get a machine to this minimal specification for around £700. Faster and more powerful is better – but note that adding extra RAM memory has more impact on running speed that stepping up to the next level of processor.

- If you want to view the videos clips that you can find on the Internet, you really need a graphics accelerator card to speed up the screen display.
- If you want to listen to the sound files that you will find, you will need a sound card. These will each add around £75 to the cost.

Your **modem** (Section 4) should be able to run at a **Baud rate** (4.4) of 9600 or 14.4k, preferably with a **data compression** (4.5) facility. This should cost around £150. If you do not have a phone socket close by your computer, you can buy an easy-to-install extension kit from any DIY store for a few pounds.

The running costs will vary hugely. They depend upon how you use the Internet, how much time you spend on-line, how fast you can transfer data over the phone, which service provider you use and whether or not you have a local connection point.

Service charges

Some service providers charge for on-line time, with a small monthly minimum. Charges are normally 5 to 10p per minute, with a monthly minimum of around £5. This is a sensible option where your main use of the Internet is to send and receive **e-mail** (2.2) or **newsgroup** (2.3) articles. As you can transfer several dozen messages in minute, your on-line time will be low.

Others providers have a flat fee with no connection time charges. Typical rates for these are around £12 - £18 per month. This is the option for those who will be playing games or browsing the **World Wide Web** (2.6) for hours at a time.

With both types of services, you may have to pay an initial registration fee, usually of around £25.

Transfer speeds

How fast you can transfer data over the phone depends upon the **Baud rate** (4.4) used by your modem and that of your service provider. At the moment, you can move data 16 times as fast over the best connections as you can over the slowest. Faster doesn't only mean less waiting, it also has direct impact on...

Telephone charges

If your provider is a long-distance phone call away, then your telephone costs will be over twice as high as for a local connection. At the time of writing, BT cheap rate charges are just under 1.5p per minute for local calls, and around 5p for long-distance calls.

● If you are just dialling up once a day to get your mail, then even a long-distance connection will only add £1 per month to your phone bill.
● If you use the Internet interactively for an hour a day, a local connection will cost upwards of £20 a month.

If you are very lucky, as we are in Southampton, you will be able to use a service provider that can be called up over the local cable phone network, which doesn't charge its for local calls in the evening.

─────────── **1.7 Summary** ───────────

● The Internet is the result of world-wide cooperation between computer networks in commercial, educational and other organisations. It is open to all – many millions have already joined, and more are joining every day.

- You may be able to can gain access to the Internet through your firm, college or university, but anyone can link in from home.
- Many of the Internet's resources can be easily used thanks to the latest graphical software.
- To set up a home terminal, you need a computer, modem and phone line; suitable software; and an account with a service provider.
- The basic hardware can be bought for around £1,000 in total; running costs depend mainly on the amount of use and whether or not you have a local phone connection.

INTERNATIONAL PHONE BILLS?

No matter where in the world you travel through the Internet, the only telephone charges are to your service provider.

2

INTERNET FACILITIES

——— 2.1 Aims of this chapter ———

When answering the question **What can I do with it?** (1.4), we looked briefly at the range of on-line activities. As the Internet is a thing of many parts, it often offers several methods for achieving the same results. Which of these you can use depends upon the nature of the connection with your service provider and the software tools that you have. As you read through the facilities outlined below, try to relate these back to the activities listed earlier.

GETTING THE TOOLS

All the software tools that you need for work on the Internet are available either from the service providers or over the Internet. The main ones, and where to get them, are listed in **ftp sources** (14.3) at the end of the book.

2.2 E-mail

Electronic mail is the simplest and the most widely used of all the Internet facilities. E-mail is mainly used for sending plain text, though it is also possible to attach graphics, sounds, word-processed documents and other data files to e-mail messages. Some people find that e-mail is the only Internet facility that they need, and there is a service provider, **WinNET** (7.8), that caters specially for them, though all providers handle e-mail.

Most e-mail is one-to-one communication, but there are also **mail lists** (9.2) that circulate messages to their members. Each of the many hundreds of lists covers a specialist interest, and almost all are open to anyone to join.

E-mail can be written and read while you are on-line, but is best managed *off-line*. This way, you are only on-line to your service for as long as it takes to transmit pre-written messages and to download incoming mail, saving this to disk. It doesn't

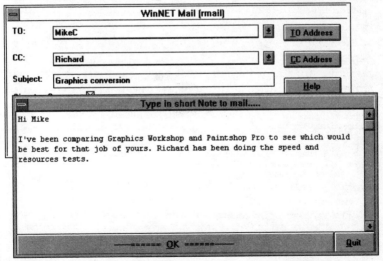

Figure 2.1 Composing a short e-mail message. The mail will be sent to the people in the To: and CC: (copies) lines.

just reduce your costs, it also avoids the possibility of losing a connection half way through writing a message, and it gives you time to check your text for typing and spelling errors first.

When sending messages, you must get the **e-mail addresses** (7.3) exactly right, or the post won't get through. There are tools to help you find addresses, though the simplest way is to ring up your contacts and ask them!

2.3 Newsgroups

These are a development of mail lists, and can be accessed by an e-mail connection. There are thousands of newsgroups, covering an amazing range of interests, activities and obsessions, from the mundane to the bizarre. Some newsgroups are very active, with hundreds of new articles every day; others have

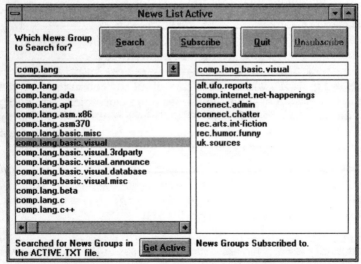

Figure 2.2 A good communications package will give you an easy way to join – and leave – newsgroups.

much lighter traffic. Some groups clearly have members with too much free time and free access to the Internet; in others, the articles are typically brief but relevant and interesting. Some groups are moderated – i.e. they have someone to edit submissions and filter out the irrelevant ones. Unmoderated groups on topics that attract obsessives can produce vast quantities of articles that are of little interest to anyone but their authors.

Sample a variety of groups, but take them a few at a time – unless you are prepared to see your mailbox and your hard disk filled with megabytes of junk!

─────── 2.4 File Transfer ───────

Throughout the Internet, there is a standard way of accessing directories on remote computers and transfering files to and from them. This is **ftp** (11.2) – file transfer protocol. It consists of a set of user commands and underlying routines to manage the safe transmission of files. You can do ftp by logging in to a remote computer and giving the commands directly, but most users now manage ftp through a Windows interface such as **WS FTP** (11.4), which takes care of all the commands for you. It is also possible – and sometimes more convenient – to do **ftp by mail** (11.7). This is done by sending a request, detailing the file you want, and where it is, to an *ftp server*. This is a computer that runs a special program to deal with such requests.

That raises the question of how you find where files are in the first place, and the solution there is **Archie** (10.2). This is a program run on certain computers – *archie servers* – that will search the Internet's archives for you.

It is worth noting that most service providers keep a bank of commonly used programs, including most of the tools that you need for Internet work, on their own computers. This is always the first place to check for files, as obtaining them from there is generally quicker and easier than searching for them elsewhere.

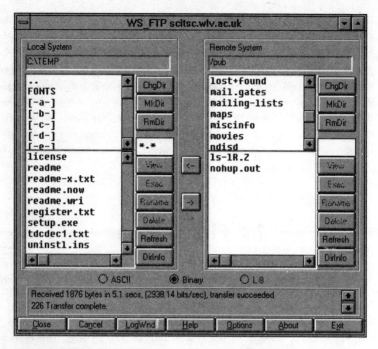

Figure 2.3 With WS_FTP, transfering files from a remote computer is as easy as moving them between directories on your own – but a lot slower!

——— 2.5 Gopherspace ———

A few years back at the University of Minnesota, they came up with *Gopher* – a pun on 'Go for' and a reference to the University mascot – designed to make it easier to find information on the Internet. **Gopher** (12.2) is a package of complementary programs that organise data and provide access to it. If you are running a Gopher program and log in to a host computer that acts as a gopher server, you will see a menu on your screen.

Selecting an item from this menu will either take you to another menu of items or display a file. The file or menu that you select may be on the same host computer, or on another one somewhere else in the world. The great mass of information on these linked computer is sometimes refered to as *Gopherspace*.

Most of the files that can be accessed through gophers are text, either plain or formatted by a word-processor, though there are also a lot of graphics, plus some videos and sounds. To be able to see and hear these, you need suitable *viewers* – software that can handle the file formats. You may well already have some programs that can be used for viewing; others can be obtained from the databanks of the Internet. A good gopher program, such as **HGopher** (6.9), will have the ability to display files in a variety of formats, and to make links to other viewers.

The menus are usually well structured, with clear indications of what each item will lead to. However, if you do not fancy tracking through the menus, there are two search programs, **Veronica** and **Jughead** (12.4), that take you directly to a topic.

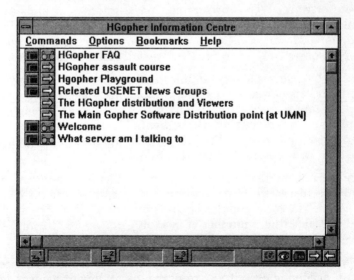

Figure 2.4 A top-level gopher menu, as accessed with Hgopher.

Out in gopherspace you can find information on every conceivable field of human knowledge, but note that the emphasis tends to be on academic interests.

—— 2.6 The World Wide Web ——

This is the newest and, for many, the most exciting aspect of the Internet. It consists of several million *pages* of information, stored on host computers throughout the world. The pages contain text, graphics, video clips, sounds and – most importantly – **hypertext links** (8.2) to other pages. Clicking on a link item calls up the related page, which may be in the same computer, or in another machine the other side of the World.

To access the World Wide Web, you need an interactive connection with your service provider, and a web browser – a program that can interpret the links and display Web pages. Like gopher software, Web browsers can pass graphics, sounds and other formatted files to viewers for display. The first two Web browsers, Mosaic and Cello, are now largely being superceded by **Netscape** (8.3) – the one that we will focus on in this book.

The Web performs a very similar function to gopher, in providing links between scattered information, but it does so in a more flexible and a more user-friendly way. It has links through to gopherspace, so that anything available there is available through a Web browser. Ftp file transfer and many newsgroups can also be accessed through the Web.

Finding information on the Web is not difficult. There are several directories, which provide structured entries into the mass of pages. The most popular of these at present is **Yahoo** (8.9). you will also find a number of **search engines** (8.12), or Web crawlers, that will track down specific topics.

People set up Web pages for many reasons – as a public service, as an academic exercise or resource, as an advertisement for

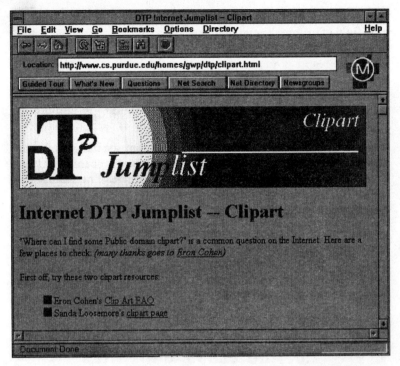

Figure 2.5 Browsing the World Wide Web with Netscape – the underlined items carry links to other pages.

their products or for themselves, or simply as a means of sharing their interests with others. As a result, some Web pages are excellent sources of information in their own right, some are treasure troves of links to other valuable pages; and some are pure trivia. You have to be selective, and you have to keep an eye on the phone bill, for Web browsing is a fascinating, but time-consuming activity.

—— 2.7 Other approaches ——

For most people, e-mail, newsgroups, ftp, gopher and the World Wide Web provide all the access to the Internet that they need, and they are the ones that we will concentrate on. There are other approaches, however, that you may want to explore as you become more experienced in using the Internet.

Telnet allows you to log in to a remote computer and use it as if your machine was directly attached to it, so you can search its directories and run programs. As most of these run the Unix operating system, you should be familiar with the essentials of Unix before attempting to telnet.

WAIS, the Wide Area Information Search tool, will trawl through indexed text files searching for those relating to defined topics. As the files are largely academic papers and technical reports, this is a tool that academics may find particularly valuable when starting to research a new topic.

—— 2.8 Addresses and URLs ——

When the Internet first got going, every site was identified by a unique number like this:

10111011011101110111011100000111010001

Most people have trouble with 32-bit binary numbers, so it was agreed to chop these numbers into 4 sets of 8 bits, and turn each into a normal decimal number, separated by dots. The one above translates to this:

193.119.97.209

These were a bit better, but still not very memorable. Fortunately, nowadays, most places have readable addresses.

Internet addresses

Every computer site that is linked to the Internet has its own unique address. This is made up of two or more names, separated by dots, and they identify the country (if not based in the US), the nature of the organisation, the organisation itself and, maybe, a particular computer or network. In the jargon these are referred to as *domains*.

Some of the major domains that you will meet are:

com   commercial
net   network provider
gov   government department
mil   military (USA)
edu   educational (USA)
ac   academic
org   non-commercial organisation
au   Australia
fr   France
fi   Finland
gr   Germany
uk   United Kingdom

Some typical examples are:
microsoft.com
A *com*mercial organisation, based in the US.

vnet.ibm.com
The *vnet* network within the IBM company.

micros.hensa.ac.uk
The computer on which the *micros* files are stored, at the University of Lancaster (*hensa*), an *ac*ademic site in the *UK*.

sunsite.unc.edu
This is a *site* sponsored by *Sun* computers, within the Univeristy of North California, an *edu*cational organisation in the US. As a major source of software and other files, this is an **ftp site** (14.3) worth knowing.

macdesign.win-uk.net

This is me, as a member of the PC User Group's WinNET. My home connection counts as a site belonging to *win-uk*, a provider of *net*work services.

N.B. These are addresses of sites only. Each individual within a site has his or her own **e-mail address** (7.3).

Uniform Resource Locators

With all the millions of files, Gopher items and Web pages that are accessible over the Internet, a standardised and systematic way of identifying them is essential. URLs provide this. There are different styles of URL for different approaches to the Internet, though they all follow the same pattern:

type://host_computer_address/directory_&_filename

Files for ftp

These always specify the path from the top to the directory containing the file. The filename is the last item on the list.

ftp://ftp.temple.edu/pub/info/funstuff/smiley.txt

This is the address of the file *smiley.txt*, which will tell you all you want to know – and a lot that you don't – about **smileys and abbreviations** (9.5) that are used in e-mail. It is in the *funstuff* directory, inside the *info* directory, inside the *pub* main directory of the *ftp* computer at *Temple* university in the US.

Web pages

Many of these are instantly recognisable from their *html* endings, which shows that they are hypertext pages.

http://sunsite.unc.edu/boutell/faq/www-faq.html

This one is a list of frequently asked questions (*faq*) and their answers, about the World Wide Web (*www*), stored in the Sun archives that we noted above.

Gopher items

Gopher URLs are the most complicated of the lot, which reflects the fact that it is more complicated to point your gopher software at a particular item, than it is to connect to a Web page or locate a file for ftp transfer.

```
gopher://gopher.ocf.berkeley.edu:70/00/gopher/gopher-www
```

The numbers after the site name identify the port that you have to connect to on the remote computer, and the nature of the item. When you get round to setting **gopher bookmarks** (12.4), this should become clearer.

2.9 Summary

- For many users, e-mail is the most useful Internet facility, as it enables them to keep in touch with friends throughout the world, at the cost of a brief phone call.
- Newsgroups are a means by which people can share ideas and knowledge. There are thousands of newsgroups, covering every conceivable interest.
- As only text files are transferred by e-mail, and in newsgroups, these facilities require only the simplest of connections to the Internet and are offered by all providers.
- Ftp allows you to download files from host computers, as long as you know their names and locations.
- Archie will find files for you.
- Gopher software give you access to a huge body of information, organised through a hierarchy of menus.
- The World Wide Web likewise gives access to masses of information, but organised in a more flexible way.
- Gopherspace, ftp and other Internet facilities can also be reached through the Web.
- Every site on the Internet has its own unique address.
- Every file and Web page has a Uniform Resource Locator, which tells you where it is and how to reach it.

ACCESS RESTRICTIONS

It will be obvious that when you are telnetting you are using resources on a remote computer; when performing a search with Archie, Veronica, WAIS or a Web crawler, you are also taking time on the host computer that holds the search program. Less obviously, downloading a file with ftp, and reading a gopher menu or a page on the Web also use the remote resources. There is a limit to how many people any computer can serve at the same time, and you will hit the limit often as you travel through the Internet. Some host systems allow only restricted access – or no access at all – to their machines during the normal working day, leaving them free for on-site students and staff; even where access is permitted, the thoughtful Internet user will try to avoid prolonged use of a remote system during the daytime. There is a certain amount of self-interest in this, as you will find that things run faster when there are fewer people trying to use a computer.

Remember that the Internet is world-wide, and that many hosts are in the USA. Mid-evening in the UK is afternoon in California and early morning in Australia!

3

DATA COMMUNICATIONS

——— 3.1 Aims of this chapter ———

When computers try to talk to each other over the phone lines, there are a number of problems to be solved. There are different forms of data within computers – plain text, formatted text of word-processors, graphics, sounds, the files created by databases, spreadsheet and other applications programs, and the programs themselves. Computers also vary, and you could probably find almost every type of computer that has been built in the last 10 years on the Internet! If these varied computers are to talk to each other, it is essential that they use common standards.

In this chapter we will be looking at the nature of computer data, and at some of the key standards that control data communications. The first two sections are for those who know little or nothing about computer data and files. If you are familiar with these concepts, skip to 3.4, *Error checking*.

3.2 Bits and Bytes

The basic unit of computer data is the **bit** – short for **binary digit**. Inside the machine, it is held as a change of voltage, or a magnetic pattern, but we think of it as either a 1 or 0. A group of 8 bits is called a **byte**, and can hold a number between 0 and 255.

Without going into details of how it works, you can use the table below to convert binary numbers into their denary (base 10) values – the ones we normally use.

For each bit that is set to 1, add in the value from the top line:

	128	64	32	16	8	4	2	1		
Binary	0	1	1	0	1	0	0	1		
Denary		64 +	32	+	8	+		1	=	105

Use this on a byte full of 1s – 11111111 – and you will get 255, which is the biggest number you can store in a byte. There are several different ways in which bytes can be put together to hold larger values, none of which need concern us.

What is important is that, though a byte will always be just a string of 1s and 0s, it can represent a character, or an instruction to the processor, or be part of a number, or of a graphic, or other form of data. What a byte of data stands for depends upon the program that is interpreting that data.

Bytes are grouped in:

    Kilobytes (Kb)   = 1024 bytes

    Megabytes (Mb) = 1024 Kb

    Gigabytes (Gb)   = 1024 Mb

With disk storage and computer memory getting cheaper, and files larger and more plentiful, even Gigabytes don't seem that large anymore. If you want to describe the quantity of data available on the Internet, you have to talk in terms of Tetrabytes (1024 Gb)!

——— 3.3 ASCII and binary files ———

We have noted that data comes in many different forms, but for Internet purposes, there is a simple division between plain ASCII text and every other sort of data (binary files). This division is based on how they can be handled. An ASCII files can be sent by **e-mail** (2.2) without any bother; binary files are normally sent transferred by other means – though they can be e-mailed after special treatment. Here is why.

ASCII (American Standard Code for Information Interchange) is the code used by almost all computers to represent letters, digits and puctuation symbols. All the characters needed for normal English/American text are in the range from 32 to 127.

Binary	Code		Binary	Code	
00100000	32	space	01000001	65	A
00100001	33	!	01000010	66	B
00100010	34	"	...	more	capitals
...	more	symbols	01011010	90	Z
00110000	48	0			
00110001	49	1	01100001	97	a
...	more	digits	...	more	letters
00111001	57	9	01111010	122	z
00111010	58	:	...	more	symbols
...	more	symbols	01111111	127	delete

Figure 3.1 Summary of the central part of the ASCII table. Note that the leftmost (8th) bit is always 0.

The codes between 0 and 31 are used for controlling the printer, the screen and communications between computers. Some of these vary, to suit the needs of different machines.

Codes above 128 – the Extended ASCII characters – are used for foreign (accented) letters, mathematical symbols and block graphics. There are several alternative Extended ASCII sets in common use, and no single standard.

Glance down the binary columns of that main ASCII set and you will note that the first bit is always 0. Plain ASCII text, sometimes called 7-bit ASCII, does not use the eighth bit, which leaves it free for **parity checks** (3.4) – a simple but effective error-checking technique, much used in data communications.

With binary files, whether they are executable programs or files from a database, spreadsheet, word-processor, graphics or sound software, all 8 bits of a byte are used. Parity checking is therefore not possible on these files, unless they have been converted into a special form, (**Binaries by mail** 7.9).

—— 3.4 Error checking ——

We all know how a poor phone line can leave us struggling to make sense of what the other person is saying. Computers suffer even more, as they lack our ability to make educated guesses at what was said. It follows that we must have ways of identifying and dealing with errors in transmissions.

Parity checks

These are our first line of defence. Parity is a simple concept. If you count up the number of bits in a byte that are set to 1, you will have either an odd or even number. For example, the byte 01010101 has 4 bits set to 1. It can be said to have *even parity*. With plain ASCII text, the eighth bit of every byte is 0. If you set this to 1, you can change the parity of the byte, without affecting the other 7 bits – the ones that carry its meaning. Take a stream of ASCII characters, set the eighth bits as necessary, and you can make all of them have even parity.

Processors have built into them the ability to check the parity of bytes, so if you pass your stream to another computer, it can easily check that they all still have even parity. If they don't, it

Char	Code	Binary	Even?	Trans'd	Rec'd	Even?	
I	73	01001001	N	11001001	11001001	Y	
N	78	01001110	Y	01001110	01001110	Y	
T	84	01010100	N	11010100	11010100	Y	
E	69	01000101	N	11000101	11000001	N	#1
R	82	01010010	N	11010010	10111010	N	#2
N	78	01001110	Y	01001110	01001101	Y	#3
E	69	01000101	N	11000101	11000101	Y	
T	84	01010100	N	11010100	11010100	Y	

Figure 3.2 Even parity. Notice how the eight (leftmost) bit is set to 1 if the byte does not have an even number of 1s, to create even parity.

Differences between Transmitted and Received bytes are <u>underlined</u>. The parity check will spot the errors in bytes #1 and #2, though #3 would pass through undetected.

knows that noise on the line has corrupted the signal, and it can ask the other computer to retransmit. If they all have even parity, it can reset the eighth bits to 0 and restore the characters.

Odd parity can be used in exactly the same way. Either can be used, as long as the modems at both ends of the line are agreed.

Figure 3.2 shows the word 'INTERNET' as it would be transmitted and received using even parity error checking. Compare the Transmitted and Received columns, and you can see that the connection must have been 'noisy' for there have been errors. Some of these (#1 and #2) will be picked up by the receiving computer, as the bytes no longer have even parity. The other (#3) will not be spotted. Two bits have been altered here, but the parity is still even.

Parity checking is not a foolproof way of spotting errors, but in practice it normally works. If a line is subject to noise, it will usually affect more than one byte, and the chances are that at least one of the errors will change the parity of its byte. Data is sent in blocks, and if there is an error on any one byte, the whole block is retransmitted.

Stop bits

An extra bit, known as the *stop bit* is normally sent after each byte to mark its end. Just to make life interesting, this bit can be 1, 1° or 2 bits long!

When setting up your modem to connect to an on-line system, you may have to specify the way that parity is used, and the nature of the stop bit. There are two methods in common use:

  8-N-1   8 Data bits, No parity, 1 Stop bit

  7-E-1   7 Data bits, Even parity, 1 Stop bit

Look out for these in **Getting on-line** (Section 5)

Checksums and CRC

As parity checks alone are not enough, and you cannot even use them with binary files where all eight bits are essential, we need additional forms of error checking.

One technique uses checksums. Put simply, here is how they work. As a block of bytes is transmitted, the modem adds their values and transmits the total at the end. The receiving modem likewise adds up the incoming bytes, and compares its total with the one sent down. If they disagree, it knows that the block has been corrupted, and it will ask for retransmission. Matching totals are not an absolute guarantee of an error-free block. It is possible for errors to cancel each other out, but this is very unlikely.

The CRC (cyclical redundancy check) method is even more reliable. It's also far more complex. Fortunately, you don't have to understand how it works, but as you will come across it, you should know why it is there.

—— 3.5 File transfer protocols ——

Protocols are agreed ways of doing things properly. There are a lot of them around in data communications, and they are essential if different types of computers are to be able to communicate with each other. There is one set of protocols that you will come across when attempting to transfer files to and from a remote computer. If you are to do it successfully, you must set your machine, and the one at the other end, to use the same protocol. This is usually not difficult – it is often only a matter of selecting one from a menu in your **communications software** (5.2), and from a menu at the remote computer.

XModem/CRC

Xmodem is one of the oldest but still widely used protocols for transferring binary files. The original version used simple checksums for error detection, but this has been largely replaced by one that uses CRC error-checking (I said you would come across it). Exactly how it works is irrelevant, but there are some points that you should note. It is relatively slow, partly because if a transmission is interrupted, the whole lot has to be sent again. It is very reliable – when all else fails, a file sent by Xmodem does get through. You can only transfer one named file at a time, and Xmodem is designed only for 8-bit file transfers.

Ymodem

Ymodem is based on Xmodem, but has the ability to transfer a group of files, specified by a wildcard, e.g. *.txt. In practice, this is not very important when working on the Internet, as you will normally be selecting individual files.

Zmodem

This is a more significant improvement on Xmodem, as it gives faster throughput and better recovery of corrupted transmissions. It is widely used, and if you have the choice, try Zmodem first.

Kermit

This is another well-established protocol, but seems to be going out of favour. One notable feature of Kermit is that is can handle binary files in 8-bit *and* 7-bit transfers, as well as ASCII text in 7-bit mode.

——————— 3.6 Handshaking ———————

One of the problems of getting different machines talking to one another is that they may run at different speeds. Handshaking is the solution. It allows the modem at the receiving end to suspend the flow of data for a moment, while it deals with what has come in. There are two main approaches, and when setting up your terminal, you may be asked to specify which to use:

Xon/Xoff   where the software sends a special code, called XOFF, to halt the flow, and an XON to restart it.

Hardware where it is left to the modems to control the flow.

Both are common. When in doubt, try Xon/Xoff first.

——— 3.7 Internet protocols ———

TCP/IP

TCP/IP (Transport Control Protocol / Internet Protocol) are strictly speaking two separate things, but the term is now used to cover a set of protocols that allow computers to share resources across the Internet. At the core are some low-level functions that control the basic interaction between computers. They wrap up data into packets for transmission and handle all the details of networking, so that higher-level protocols can treat the network connection as if it were a direct phone line.

At the higher level are protocols that provide applications for users. Two keys ones are:

Ftp (File Transfer Protocol) (2.4 and 11.2) handles access to directories and files on remote computers.

Telnet (2.7) governs ways of working on remote computers.

Your service provider must offer a TCP/IP connection if you want interactive access to the Internet.

SLIP

The Serial Line Internet Protocol works on top of TCP/IP, and allows data – of any type – to be communicated. When you have a **SLIP connection** (6.2), your computer becomes a part of the Internet. It can then handle incoming graphics as easily as ASCII text – as far as SLIP is concerned, all data is the same. If you want to get into the World Wide Web, you must have a SLIP driver – a program that handles a SLIP connection. They are not difficult to find or use. One is built into **Trumpet Winsock** (Section 6), a shareware program for Windows.

——— 3.8 Terminal emulation ———

On a multi-user computer system, the users typically work at *dumb terminals*. These consist of screens and keyboards, with no processing power of their own. The commands and data that the user types in are echoed on the screens, but sent to a large central computer for processing. The simplest way to connect to a remote computer, it to make your computer emulate a terminal.

Note that this is the simplest only in *technical* terms, not in terms of usage. Terminals are text-only interfaces. You type in your commands or data when prompted, and the computer at the other end sends its replies, with the lines of text scrolling steadily up the screen.

Some terminals allow the cursor to be positioned so that text can be laid out properly on the screen; some permit the use of

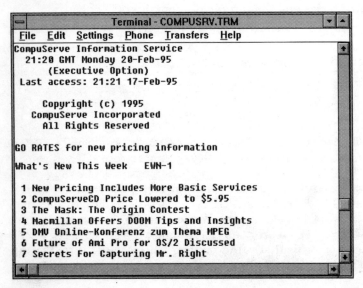

Figure 3.3 Logging in to CompuServe from Windows Terminal, using VT-100 emulation.

simple block graphics and colour, but none gives you those pull-down menus or buttons that make computer work so easy.

Note also that the fact that facilities are there does not mean that they will be used, and many on-line systems stick to simple text.

Modern communications software packages offer ways of connecting that are far simpler to work with. However, you will have to use terminal emulation if you want to log in to a remote computer, and you may need it to make the initial contact with a new service.

There are four types of terminal emulation in common use:

TTY stands for TeleTYpe, and gives a plain, scrolling display

DEC VT-52 and **VT-100** emulate two of DEC's more popular terminals produced; both permit cursor positioning

ANSI uses the American National Standards control characters to give colour and block graphics, as well as cursor control, allowing fairly fancy screens to be produced.

If the service does not specify a type, try ANSI or VT-100.

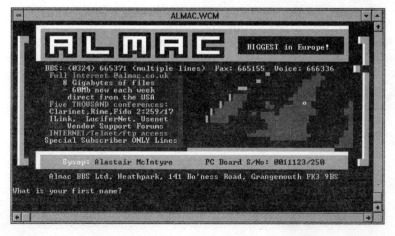

Figure 3.4 Logging in to Almac using ANSI emulation, in Works.

3.9 Summary

- The basic unit of data is a bit. 8 bits make a byte, and a byte can hold a character, number or many other forms of data.

- Data is normally measured in Kilobytes and Megabytes.

- ASCII text only uses 7 bits in a byte, leaving the eighth free for error-checking. Binary files use all 8 bits. In practice, this means that you can send plain text by (7-bit) e-mail, but not graphics, programs or other binaries.

- The simplest form of error-checking uses the parity bit. Checksums and CRC provide more reliable methods of detecting errors in transmissions.

- When transferring files, you will normally have to specify which protocol to use. Xmodem and Z modem are the ones most commonly used at present. You will also have to set the type of handshaking that is used for flow control.

- If your service provider offers a TCP/IP connection to the Internet, this will give you interactive access. You will need a SLIP driver, like Trumpet Winsock, to manage the connection at your end.

- Terminal emulation is the simplest way to interact with a remote computer.

4

MODEMS

—— 4.1 Aims of this chapter ——

At present, a modem is an essential item for anyone who wants to get into the Internet – or any other data communication system for that matter. But why?

This chapter aims to answer that question by looking at how modems transmit data over the phone lines. It also covers the more practical questions of how they are controlled, what to look for when buying a modem, and how to install them.

With a standard PC, a standard modem and a user-friendly service provider, fitting and using your modem should present no problems. But not everything is standard and user-friendly!

COMMUNICATION WITHOUT MODEMS?

You may be wondering why I said that modems are needed *at present*. Eventually, all phone lines will be digital, allowing computers to talk to each other directly – but not yet.

—— 4.2 Digital and analogue ——

Inside a computer, data travels as a digital signal, with the current flipping between (typically) +6 volts for 1 and -6 volts for 0, producing a square waveform.

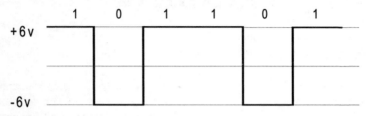

Figure 4.1 Representation of a digital signal

In the phone lines, the signal is *analogue*, varying continuously, and producing a curved wave. This works well for voice communications, as the electrical signal is a simple reflection of the sound waves we create when we talk.

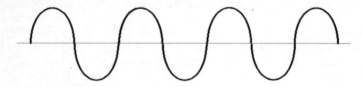

Figure 4.2 Representation of an analogue signal.

The process of imposing a digital signal on an analogue wave is known as *modulation*, and equipment that does it is a modulator/demodulator, or *modem*. How it works needn't concern us. The important point is that, though they all work in basically the same way, there are differences in the speed and efficiency with which they can transmit and receive data. They also differ in how they are connected to the computer and to the phone line – and in cost! We will start with these more visible differences.

4.3 Modem types

There is a wide range of modems and they vary in a number of ways – how they connect to the phone lines, how they connect to your computer, how fast they can work, what extra facilities they offer, and how much they cost.

Direct wired and audio

A *direct wired modem* has a connector that plugs into a standard telephone wall socket. A matching socket on the modem takes the phone connection, so that it can still be used for conversation. The modem does not have to be on for the phone to work – the wiring simply loops through it and out to the wall socket. If it doesn't say otherwise on the advert, the modem is direct-wired.

The audio variety of modem converts its signal into sound and links to the phone via a pair of cups into which the phone handset fits. These were common a few years ago, but have been largely replaced by the more reliable direct-wired type. They are now mainly owned by portable computer users who may not be able to get access to a plug-in socket on their travels.

Internal or External

Internal, or **c**ard *modems* are designed to fit into an expansion slot on a PC. They have the advantages of being slightly cheaper than their external equivalents (as there is no box to pay for) and of taking up no space on your desk. Of the many types of cards that you can add to your PC, these are normally about the easiest to install. See **Installing an internal modem** (4.7).

External modems are typically around 8 inches square and 1° high. They can sit on top of your computer's box, or be tucked away beneath your phone. They normally have LED displays or indicator lights on the front panel, but for most of us these will be more decorative than useful. **Installing an external modem** (4.7) is generally just a matter of plugging it into the phone line and into a free **serial port** (4.6) at the back of your computer.

———— 4.4 Baud rates ————

The main way in which modems vary is in the speeds that they can process data. This is measured in its *Baud rate,* which is approximately the number of bits per second. There are certain agreed standard rates, starting at 300 Baud, with 2400 and 9600 being the most commonly used at the time of writing. The faster your modem, the less time you have to wait for information to come down the line – and the lower your telephone bills. But there are practical limits. You can only run your modem at the same speed as the one at the other end of the line, and reliability tends to decrease at higher speeds.

In practice, if you want to get on to the **World Wide Web** (2.4 and Section 8), you need a modem capable of at least 9600 Baud. Anything slower will create unacceptable delays in receiving pictures and the larger text files that are found on the Web. If you only intend to use e-mail based services, a slower modem will do. You may also find that the local connections offered by some service providers only run at 2400 Baud.

If you are not sure of the Baud rate of a modem, but have its V number, you can work it out from that. The V numbers relate to the standards set by the ITU (International Telegraphic Union). This has recently taken over the role from the CCITT (Consulatant Committee on International Telephony and Telegraphy). You may still come across references to CCITT standards. The ones below relate to Baud rates. There are other V standards covering error correction, data compression and other aspects of data communications.

ITU / CCITT	Baud rate	
V22	1200	
V22bis	2400	#1
V32	9600, 4800	
V32bis	14.4k.12000, 9600, 7200, 4800	
V34 or V.Fast	as V32bis + 28.8k	
V42	as V34 + higher	#2

#1   bis means half. The standards were originally written in French

#2   Data compression (below) can make its effective rate over 100k

Figure 4.3 V standards and Baud rates.

—————— 4.5 Data compression ——————

The Baud rate is only one factor in determining the overall speed of data transmission. The other key factor is data compression. You have probably seen how Stacker or Drivespace can double the storage capacity of a disk, or how PKZIP can scrunch three or four Megabytes of files onto a floppy. In essence, they work by replacing sequences of identical bytes with a single copy of the byte and a count of how many there are. A line of spaces (ASCII code 32) might appear in the original file as:

32 32 32 32 32 32 32 32 32 32

In the compressed file they are replaced by:

10 32

With 2 bytes replacing the 10, this gives a compression of 80%.

It is worth noting that compression does not always produce smaller files or faster throughput. A file in which there is little of no repetition cannot be compressed significantly. Small files may even grow larger, as extra data must be added to identify the type of compression. Trying to compress files that have already been compressed will also often result in a larger file.

In general, you can get compression of around 50% on text files, rising to over 90% on some types of graphics, but falling to as little as 5% on executable (program) files.

Similar data compression techniques can be used to increase the throughput of a modem. The commonly used standards covering this are V.42*bis* and MNP(Microcom Network Protocol) – this has several classes, with MNP 10 being the most sophisticated. How effective any of them they are depends to some extent upon the nature of the data being transmitted. As most of the data that you will access over the Internet will be either text or graphics, both of which pack down, a modem which can handle both V.42*bis* and MNP 10 data compression protocols is a good investment.

It is crucial that the modems at both ends of the line operate at the same speed and use the same protocols. Fortunately for us, most modern modems can handle a range of speeds and both compression techniques. They can also negotiate with each other to agree how they should communicate.

—————— 4.6 Serial ports ——————

Within the computer, data travels in *parallel*, with the 8 bits of a byte travelling simultaneously down a set of 8 parallel wires, known as a *bus* (or 16 bits down a 16 wire bus, or 32 bits down a 32-wire bus, depending upon the type of computer.) Printers are also usually connected by parallel cables. If you examine

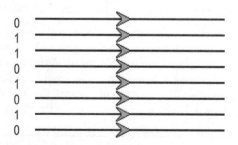

Figure 4.4 Representation of a byte, 01101010, travelling over a parallel connection.

one of these cables, you will find it actually has more than 8 wires, as extra ones are needed or control and checking purposes.

Phone lines only have three wires, and only one of these carries data. To get data into and out of a computer on a single wire, it must travel in serial form – one bit after another. The end of each byte is usually marked by a **Stop bit** (3.4).

....Stop 01101010...

Figure 4.5 Representation of serial transmission.

All modern computers have one or more serial ports to which you can attach devices that take data in serial form. These are built to the RS232 standard, and some are present as sockets at the rear of the machine, marked *RS232 interface*, or *Serial port*. On a PC, there are up to 4 serial ports, identified as COM1, COM2, COM3 and COM4. Some of these exist as external sockets, others as connections within the computer, picked up from the expansion slots.

Modem connections follow the same RS232 standard, and the modem may be plugged in to any unused port on the computer. In practice, it is likely that your mouse (another serial device) is using COM1, so the next free one is COM2. Most modems come ready configured to use this port, so it is not normally something you have to worry about.

> The key point to note is that if you only have one serial port on the back of your computer, and it already has the mouse plugged into it, you cannot use it to connect an external modem.

Jumper settings

If you do have to use an alternative port, you will probably have to change jumper settings in your modem. Jumpers are connectors that fit over a pair of vertical pins mounted in a small block. There may be several pairs of pins, as shown below, or three or four in a single row. Moving the jumper changes the circuit at the hardware level, and fixes a new setting. As they are so small, it is a fiddly job, best managed with a pair of thin-nosed pliers or a small screwdriver. Check your modem's manuals for details, and disconnect the modem (or the computer if the modem is internal) from the mains before you start.

If you reset the jumpers for the COM port, you will also have to reset those for the IRQ (Interrupt ReQuest). These, and the port addresses normally follow this pattern:

COM port	IRQ	Address
1	IRQ4	3F8-3FF
2	IRQ3	2F8-2FF
3	IRQ4	3E8-3EF
4	IRQ3	2E8-3EF

Reset the jumper according to your modem's manual, then when you have the computer up and runing again, go into Windows and open the **Ports** section of the **Control panel**.

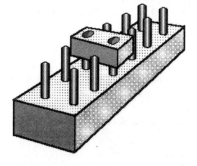

Figure 4.6 A jumper block – take care not to bend the pins if you have to switch the jumper.

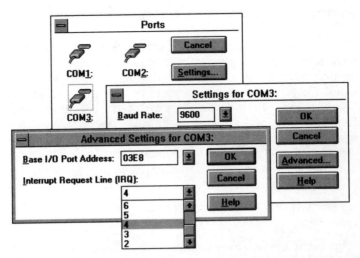

Figure 4.7 The Advanced Settings dialog box that opens from the Ports Control panel. New settings can be selected from the lists. Only change these if you really have to!

From here, select the COM port to which you have assigned the modem, open its **Settings** dialog box and go through to **Advanced Settings**. In this you can check that the IRQ and port addresses match those in the table. If need be, select the correct ones from the drop-down lists.

4.7 Installation

Installing an internal modem

All being well, the process is simply:

1 Undo the retaining screws and slide off the PC's cover
2 Unscrew and remove the blanking strip from a free slot
3 Slip the phone connection through the opening at the end of the slot

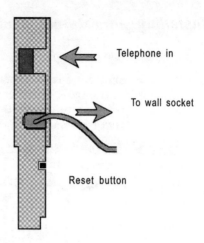

Figure 4.8 Typical back panel of an internal modem. If your phone is connected through the modem, it can still be used normally whether the computer is on or off.

Telephone in

To wall socket

Reset button

4 Push the modem card into place and fit the securing screw
5 Replace the PC's cover
6 Plug the connection into your phone socket
7 If you want to keep the phone connected, plug its line into the socket on the modem card
8 Test it with your **comms software** (5.2).

With a modern PC and a standard modem, you shouldn't have any problems, but if you do, there are three likely causes:

● The modem card has not been pushed fully down into the slot – push firmly and make sure it is bedded in along its full length.

● You are trying to connect to a **Serial port** (4.6) that is in use – probably by a mouse, though printers are sometimes connected through a serial port.

● There is a low level collision between the modem and another expansion card. The order in which cards sit in the slots affects the way they are handled by the computer. Moving the modem to a different slot may well solve it.

Installing an external modem

This should be even simpler.

1 Plug the serial lead into the socket marked **RS232** or **Serial port** at the back of the computer.
2 Connect up to the phone wall socket.
3 Reconnect your phone through the modem.

——— 4.8 The AT command set ———

The AT command set, developed by the Hayes company for their modems, have become the de facto standard. Any modem which claims Hayes-compatibility can use these commands.

The commands are used to dial and hang up the phone, set the type of data compression and error-correction used, control the display of error messages, and similar things. With a good, standard modem and well-configured, user-friendly software you may never need to define them yourself. But just in case you do, here is an overview of what they do and how they work.

● All command lines start with AT, short for ATtention, to alert the modem that new instructions are coming.
● Almost all consist of single-letter codes. Some are preceded by a & % or \ symbol; some are followed by a digit to select an option.
● A command line may include several commands, which can be separated by spaces.

The most commonly used commands are shown in Table 4.1

Examples:

ATDT 0171-490 8881

Dial this number using Tone dial. Note that the modem will ignore spaces and hyphens.

Code	Meaning
D	Dial, followed by **T** or **P** and the phone number
T	Tone dialling (used on all modern exchanges)
P	Pulse dialling
F 0	Auto speed select
H 0	on Hook (Hang-up) – **H** does the same
M 0	disable the speaker
M 1	enable the speaker while dialing, then disable it when the connection is established. This is the best, as you can hear when you are connected properly
M 2	enable speaker throughout a session – a noisy option
Q 0	enable error messages
Q 1	disable error messages
S	Set registers. These contain the values of certain control characters, how long to wait before ringing, or hanging up. They rarely need attention – if they do, see your modem manual for details.
V 1	verbose (full text) error messages
Z	Reset modem
&C 1	activate Data Carrier Detect when there is an incoming carrier signal
&D 2	Hang up if DTR (Data Terminal Ready) signal is lost
\G 0	Use XON/XOFF flow control – ignored if error-correction is active
\N 0	no error-correction
\N 2	reliable mode – only connect if error-correction possible
\N 3	try to use error-correction, but connect anyway if the remote modem can't handle it
%C 0	no data compression
%C 3	automatic selection of data compression method
+++	Escape (end session)

Table 4.1 The core AT commands.

AT Q0 V1 &C1 &D2

This is a typical setup string – the sequence of commands sent to the modem when it starts up. It enables error messages (Q0), in verbose mode (V1), and leaves it to the modem to negotiate the error correction (&C1) and data compression (&D2)methods.

ATZ

This returns the modem to its normal settings – there will be a button somewhere on your modem which does the same job.

——————— 4.9 Summary ———————

- Modems convert data into a suitable form for transmission by telephone. They may be wired directly into the phone line, or communicate via audio signals.

- Direct-wired modems can be fitted internally as an expansion card, or be a separate external unit.

- Speed of data transfer is measured by the Baud rate. A faster modem may cost a little more to buy, but will be cheaper to run, as on-line time costs money (for most of us).

- Data compression techniques can improve the throughput of data, further reducing on-line time and costs.

- A modem connects to its computer through a serial port.

- Installation of a modern modem is usually straightforward, though there can be problems when the default port is already in use.

- Most modems are Hayes-compatible, and respond to the standard AT commands.

5

GETTING ON-LINE

5.1 Aims of this chapter

Putting the hardware together is just the first stage of setting up your terminal. You also need communications software and a service provider to give you a link into the Internet.

You should already have some basic communications software – it is often bundled with modems, and if you have Windows, then you have Terminal. You can use the basic software to connect to (some) services and explore what they have to offer, before committing yourself to one or the other. You can also use it to sign up with a service and download their own special software – though given the time it takes to download some packages, you make prefer to have it sent to you.

You do not have to use your service provider's software, but it will make life much easier. It will normally be ready configured for use, and have simple means of accessing all their facilities.

We start this chapter with an overview of what communications software does, then go on-line with Terminal, using it to capture text and download files. (If software was bundled with your modem, load it up and see how it compares.)

WINDOWS 95 USERS

In Windows 95, Terminal is replaced by Hyperterminal, and the whole business of getting on-line is made much simpler by the in-built links to the Microsoft Network

---

—— 5.2 Communications software ——

Communications software may sound as if it is complex, but in fact it performs simple functions, and is relatively easy to write – which is perhaps why you so often find basic comms software bundled with other packages, or given away with modems.

At the very least, your software should be able to:

- pass commands to the modem, and control the phone.
- offer some form of **terminal emulation** (3.8).
- manage the connection when you are on-line.
- allow you to transfer **binary files** (3.3) and ASCII text.

It should also:

- store the phone numbers and details of your services.
- let you send text files, and store incoming text as files.
- handle a variety of **file transfer protocols** (3.5).

——— 5.3 Windows Terminal ———

Terminal meets most of the requirements listed above, though it offers only a limited choice of file transfer protocols. However, it performs well enough to let you get on-line and explore a little. If you have Windows,

Terminal

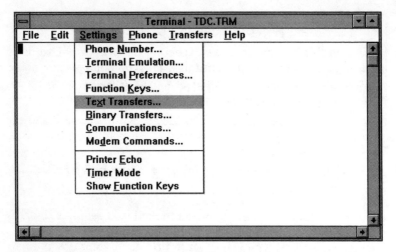

Figure 5.1 The Terminal screen, with the Settings menu open.

run Terminal now, and set it up to link to *The Direct Connection*, one of the few service providers that allows non-members to browse – albeit in a limited way. Its settings are given in the following pages.

Most of the Terminal screen is a blank space. When you are online, whatever you type will be echoed to here, while it is being sent down the line, and the remote computer's output appears here. Once the text reach the bottom of the screen, new text makes the lines scroll upwards. They are stored in a buffer, and you can go back over the text, during or after the session. By default, this buffer is 100 lines long – just over 4 screensful. As you can easily go beyond this limit is just a few minutes, you may wish to set a larger value so that you go over your session afterwards, to review what happened.

A new connection starts with the *Settings* menu. Some of these can be left at their defaults, but others do need attention.

Phone Number

This handles the number, as expected, but also what to do if you can't get through. The number may be engaged, or noise on the line may corrupt the signal during the first crucial seconds when the modems are establishing their protocols.

The *Timeout* values specifies how long to wait between dialling and giving up if you cannot make the connection. Patience is an essential virtue when working on-line, but if you can't get through in 45-60 seconds, you should give up and try again.

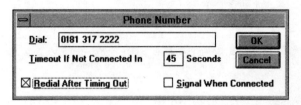

Figure 5.2 Check the Auto-redial box to keep trying a poor line. The number shown here is for the Direct Connection.

Communications

These must be tuned to your system and to that of your service.

The *Baud Rate* should be as fast as your modem can send and the service can accept – though note that Terminal does not support the 14.4k rate. Most services run at 9600 on their main nodes, but local connections are often only 2400.

The *Data Bits*, *Parity* and *Stop Bit* are taken together. There are two combinations in common use, often shown by abbreviations:

8-N-1 = 8 Data Bits, No Parity, 1 Stop Bit
7-E-1 = 7 Data Bits, Even Parity, 1 Stop Bit

The *Connection* is the **Serial Port** (4.6) you are using, and will typically be COM 2.

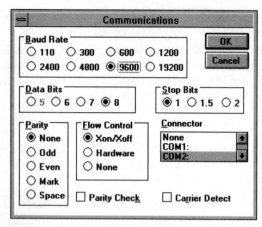

Figure 5.3 Terminal's Communications panel, showing the settings for the Direct Connection. Your Baud rate and Connection may be different.

Terminal Preferences

Cursor, Columns, Font and *Scroll bars* are a matter of choice, but other aspects can have more impact on your work.

Figure 5.4 The Terminal Preferences. Click on the check boxes to turn them on ☒ or off ☐, and on radio buttons to select ⦿ one option in each set.

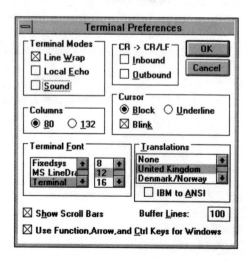

Increase the *Buffer lines* for a more complete record of a session – 300 to 400 lines should be enough.

In the *Terminal Modes*, turn on *Text Wrap* to stop long lines disappearing off the edge of the window. If, when you get on-line, you cannot see what you type, turn *Local Echo* on. If your lines of typing appear twice, then *Local Echo* should be turned off.

CR > CR / LF converts a Carriage Return to a Carriage Return + Line Feed. If lines of incoming text overwrite each other, turn the *Inbound* on. The *Outbound* should normally be left off.

Modem Commands

The *Dial* command must be changed to ATDP if you are on an old Pulse-driven telephone system.

Leave the *Modem* at Hayes, unless you have one of the other named modems.

With any luck, the other settings will work without alteration. If you cannot get a good connection, then you may have to read your modem's manual and the **At Command Set** (4.8)

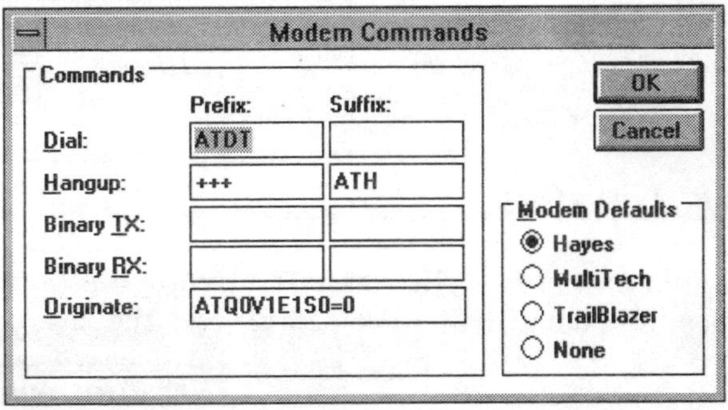

Figure 5.5 The default Modem Commands work well on most systems.

Text Transfers

The only essential here is to check that the *Flow Control* is set to Standard, using Xon/Xoff **Handshaking** (3.6). It is a good idea to set the *Word Wrap* for outgoing text at 80 columns or less.

Figure 5.6 Turning on Word Wrap for outgoing text is a courtesy to the people to whom you send e-mail, as they may not be able to Word Wrap incoming text.

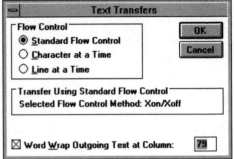

Terminal Emulation

This can usually be left at the default DEC VT 100. Only use a different one if the service provider specifically recommends it.

Figure 5.7 You may never need to bother with the Terminal Emulation dialog box .

Binary Transfers

Terminal supports two **file transfer protocols** (3.5) for binary files. Xmodem/CRC is the default and the best choice of these.

Figure 5.8 The Binary Transfers dialog box, opened from the Settings menu.

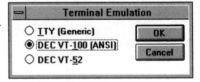

Saving Settings

Having spent all this time working through the Settings panels, you will not want to do it all again, so save them now. Pull down the *File* menu, select *Save As* and type in a name that will remind you of the service provider you have tuned to. Terminal will add a .TRM extension to the filename. Next time you want to start a sesion, use *File - Open* to get the settings back.

—————— 5.4 Before you start ——————

A few words of advice before you start working on-line:

● Don't try to run before you can walk. There's a lot to learn about the range of facilities available, the way services work and how to get the best out of your own system. If you see 'information overload' looming, log off, hang up the phone, and think about what you have learnt so far, and what you need to find out before you next go on-line.

● If you want to study incoming text properly, but would like to keep your phone bills down, then try **Capturing Text** (5.6) to a file.

● Be prepared to wait, whenever you are on-line. There will be delays, even with a fast modem. The remote computer is probably dealing with many other users as well as you. A poor telephone line will also slow things down, as the same packet of data may have to be sent several times before it gets through successfully.

● Don't wait forever. If you have had no response after around 30 seconds, it is likely that you have lost the connection. It happens – learn to live with it!

5.5 Logging in

When you want to get on-line, pull down the *Phone* menu and select *Dial*. Terminal will send the Originate string to set up the modem, then run the ATD command to dial. These are echoed to the screen. You should hear the dialling sequence on your PC's speaker, followed by whistling and chirrupping as your modem tries to establish a link with the one at the other end.

You know you are getting through when you see the CONNECT message followed by the Baud rate that is being used. Shortly after, you will see the **login** prompt from the remote computer.

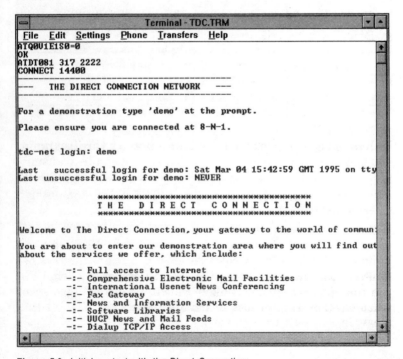

Figure 5.9 Initial contact with the Direct Connection.

It is waiting for you to enter your user name. If you dialled The Direct Connection, enter 'demo' to find out more about their service. (They will also want to find out more about you – but there is no pressure to register as a member.)

When you see the opening menu – or any of the later ones – make a choice by typing a number or letter at the prompt and pressing [Enter]. Notice that there is always an option to return to the previous menu, so you can backtrack and explore another branch.

When you have finished exploring, type 'OFF' at any prompt to log off from The Direct Connection, then use *Phone - Hangup* to end the phone call.

> There is no standard way to log off. You will find OFF, BYE, EXIT, LOGOFF, QUIT used on different services .

——————— 5.6 Text Transfers ———————

Unless you have an extremely slow modem and a very fast brain, you can neither read nor write as fast as text can be transmitted down the line. So, if you want to keep your on-line and phone charges to a minimum, the trick is to work off-line as much as possible.

If there is incoming text that needs careful reading, it can be saved as a file, as it comes in, and read later when you have hung up. If you will be writing at length, prepare the text beforehand and save it as a file. When you are on-line, that file can then be sent without delay. We will return to this aspect when we take a closer look at **Off-line Working** (7.7). At this stage, let's concentrate on saving incoming text.

Capturing text

If you want a permanent copy of a block of incoming text, you can capture it to a file – but only as it comes in, not afterwards. Here's how to do it in Terminal.

1 Just before you give the command that will start the flow of text, open the *Transfers* menu and click *Receive Text file*.

2 At the dialog, select the directory in which to store the file, make sure that it will be saved as a text file and give it a name.

3 Click *OK* to close the dialog box.

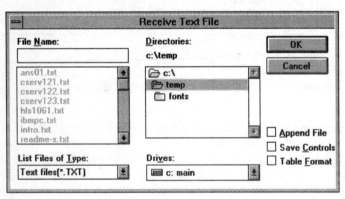

Figure 5.10 The Receive Text file dialog. Save text as .TXT files.

4 Tell the remote computer to start sending text. Everything that is send down the line from then on will be stored in that file. The Byte count in the status bar at the bottom of the screen keeps track of the size of the incoming text.

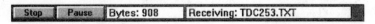

5 When you have got all you want, click the ▢Stop▢ button.

When you are off-line, use Write, Notepad or your normal word-processor to read the file.

5.7 Binary Transfers

The ability to download programs and other files from wherever you find them, whenever you want to, is one of the treats of the Internet. For getting files from distant sites, you will use an **ftp** (11.2) program, or download your **files from the Web** (11.6); but there is usually a large bank of software on the computer of your service provider. This is where you should look first for Winsock (Section 6) and the other programs that you will need for World Wide Web work. It is also where you will find any software that has been specially written for use on that service – such asWinCIM and DOSCIM for **CompuServe** (14.2) and WinTools for **WinNET Mail** (14.2). These can be downloaded easily enough with Terminal or other basic communications software.

Downloading Binary Files

Though every service has its own particular way of doing things, and its own way of organising its files, the route to the service's own communications package is normally well signposted. Go for that. Once you have it installed and running, working on-line will be much easier.

1 Pick your way through the menus or prompts to locate the file that you want to download.

2 You will be prompted for the transfer protocol to use. Specify the best you have – *XModem*, if you are using Terminal, or *Zmodem* if you are using a comms package that supports it.

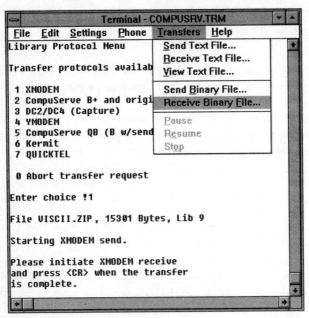

Figure 5.11 Downloading a binary file through Terminal.

3 Open the *Transfers* menu and select *Receive Binary File*. This takes you to a dialog where you set the directory and type in the filename, then click *OK*.

4 Press **[Enter]** (or whatever key is specified by the service) to tell the remote computer to start sending the file.

5 Go and make a cuppa. There is nothing else to do for a while. Services' comms packages are typically at least 500Kb and sometimes over a Megabyte. If you are running at 14400 Baud, you can download about 1k a second, or 15 to 20 minutes per Megabyte. At 9600 Baud, 1 Mb will take nearly half an hour. At 2400 Baud, large files will take a very expensive amount of phone time to download.

6 Your comms software and the remote computer will both recognise the end of the file when they reach it, so you don't have to do anything to turn off the receive. Just keep an eye out for the message that tells you transfer is done.

ZIPPED FILES

Many of the files available over the Internet are ZIPped –
compressed with PKZIP. This can reduce file sizes, and
therefore transfer times, by anything from 10% to 90%.
You will need PKUNZIP to uncompress them. You should
be able to find a copy of this shareware program in the
main file bank of your service provider.

5.8 Selecting a Service

Before you can go much further in your practical explorations
of the Internet, you need an account with a service provider.
When deciding which one, the key considerations should be:

● Do you mainly want the e-mail and newsgroup facilities,
with some file transfer, or access to the World Wide Web
and other interactive facilities?

● Is the provider local, or with a good local access point?

● What additional services does the provider offer to its
members, and how much might you use them?

● Can you try before you buy?

We have arranged free trial accounts with CompuServe and
the PC User Group. Between them, they offer three different
types of service, each with its own advantages and disadvantages. CompuServe has a comprehensive information service
for its members in addition to full mail, newsgroup, ftp and
World Wide Web access to the Internet. The PC User Group
runs two services – WinNET mail, an off-line e-mail and
newsgroup facility, and CONNECT, a fully interactive connection to the Internet.

Some other services also offer limited access, or a short period of free use to prospective members.

There are fuller details of these and a list of other **UK service providers** (14.1) at the end of this book.

Either CompuServe and the PC User Group could be a good place to start. They are both well-established organisations, and in their data banks you can find all the software tools that you need to work on the Internet. If you have a local service that will provide you with a good set of tools, that is an attractive alternative.

———————— 5.9 Summary ————————

- To get on-line, you need communications software and an account with an service provider.

- If you have Windows, you already have basic communications software in Terminal. This provides a simple means of setting up the connection and managing the link on-line.

- Before you can connect to a remote computer, you must specify the phone number, and select the communications settings.

- Terminal's buffer stores (some of) your session, and incoming text can be saved to a file for reading at leisure later.

- You can make your initial contact with many service providers through Terminal, and download their software if you join.

6

WINSOCK

6.1 Aims of this chapter

If you want to go Web browsing, or do any interactive work on the Internet, you really need a SLIP connection to your service provider and Trumpet Winsock on your machine – there are alternative approaches, but this is the best choice for those readers working from their PCs. This chapter focuses on setting up Winsock, and takes an initial look at four commonly used Winsock *clients* – software applications that run on top of the Winsock/SLIP base.

JARGON JUMPING

Apologies in advance for the jargon, but I cannot avoid it here. You *can* avoid it if you like. If you are happy to use Winsock, without worrying about what it is or how it works, jump straight to **Setting up Winsock** (6.3).

—— 6.2 SLIP and Winsock ——

SLIP

SLIP stands for Serial Line Internet Protocol, and controls the way that computers can exchange data on the Internet.

With SLIP, you are no longer limited to ASCII text, but can also handle *IP packets*. These Internet Protocol data packets are the basic units of the Internet. Each consists of a chunk of data – ASCII or binary, the type is irrelevant – accompanied by the addresses of the sending and receiving computers, along with various error-checking and network control bits. Files are split into packets before being sent, and reassembled on receipt. A program that handles these packets is known as a *packet driver*.

The point of splitting a file into packets is this. If a file is transferred as a single unit, once transfer has started, nothing else can happen over that connection until the whole file has been sent. When transferred as a set of small, discrete units, a number of files can travel down the same line, their packets interspliced with each other. With a SLIP connection and suitable software, you can download a file with ftp, read newsgroup articles, and access several Web pages simultaneously. The only limits are your computer's capability to run multiple applications and the amount of data of your link can handle. A reasonably powerful PC with 4 or more Mb of RAM, and a V.32bis (14,000 Baud) modem should be able to manage several transfers at a time.

PPP

PPP is Point to Point Protocol and serves the same function, in much the same way, as SLIP. It will also allow you to dial in to your service provider and get direct access to the Internet through them.

Trumpet Winsock

Trumpet Winsock is a Windows Sockets 1.1 compatible TCP/IP stack. (TCP/IP stands for Transfer Control Protocol/Internet Protocol and governs the way that data is transmitted over the Internet.) It manages your end of a SLIP or PPP connection, taking care of the underlying networking details, and acting as a base for client applications.

In practical terms, this means that when starting a session, you first use Winsock to dial in to your service provider. Once you have established the connection, you can minimize Winsock out of the way, and run your application program – **Eudora** (7.10), **Netscape** (8.3) or whatever. At the end of the session, you restore Winsock and log off from your provider.

——— 6.3 Setting up Winsock ———

Winsock is shareware and is widely available. When you set up your SLIP/PPP account, your service provider will either send you a copy, or direct you to their file banks to download one. You may receive it as TRUMPET.ZIP, or as a self-extracting ZIPped file – one that uncompresses its enclosed files when you run it. If you have a thoughtful service provider, you will receive a complete package that will install Winsock and its clients on to your system, along with detailed instructions on how to set things up. If they exist, use them and skip the rest of this section. If not, work from the following notes – they should do the job.

Create a directory called TRUMPET or WINSOCK, then decompress the ZIP file into the new directory with PKUNZIP. Run Window's File Manager and you should see these files:

● **WINSOCK.DLL** – this should be moved into your WINDOWS or WINDOWS\SYSTEM directory.

- **TCPMAN.EXE** – the main program. It should be installed as an icon in a Program Manager group. This must be set up before it can be used.

Tcpman

You might also have some or all of these:

- **WINPKT.COM** – this is a packet driver, and not necessary on later versions of Winsock, where the packet driver is built into the software.
- **HOSTS** – a list of host computers that you link up to often. This can be added to if you like, once you have started to use Winsock.
- **PROTOCOL** – the Internet protocols recognised by Winsock.
- **SERVICES** – a list of Internet services and their codes.
- **LOGIN.CMD** – a script that Winsock will run through when you log in. This will need editing.
- **BYE.CMD** – a log out script. This should not need editing.

This is a two (and possibly three) stage process as you must set up the TCPMAN software and the login script.

TCPMAN

To set up TCPMAN, you must get some magic numbers from your service provider. (They are *magic* because they do the trick, but how is too complicated to explain!)

You need to know:

- **Default name server or DNS**
- **MTU**
- **TCP/RWIN**
- **TCP/MSS**

You may also need your own **IP address** number. With some services, you will not have a fixed number; instead, a new number will be dynamically allocated to you when you log on. With these to hand, run TCPMAN and select *File – Setup*.

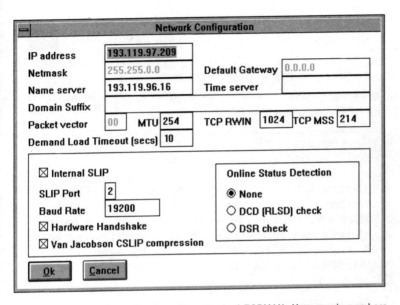

Figure 6.1 The Network Configuration panel of TCPMAN. Your magic numbers will be different from mine.

At the *Network Configuration* dialog box, type your magic numbers into the boxes in the top half. If you do not have your own **IP address**, leave it set to 0.0.0.0.

The **Demand load Timeout** is how long it should wait when trying to connect to a remote host – set it to 5 or 10 seconds.

In the bottom half:

● the **SLIP port** is the same as your serial (COM) port.
● the **Baud rate** should be as fast as possible – and with data compression, you may be able to run faster than the nominal speed of your modem. My 14,400 modem runs happily at 19,200 over the SLIP connection.
● check the **Internal SLIP** box. This takes care of the packet driver side of things.
● check **Hardware handshake**. Winsock will not work with Xon/Xoff **handshaking** (3.6).

- check **Van Jacobson compression** for faster throughput.
- the **On-line Status Detection** can be left at *None*.

Click *OK* to close the panel, then exit from TCPMAN. You will find that a new file, named TRUMPWSK.INI, has been created in the directory. The settings held in here will take effect when you next run the program.

BUG FIX!

There is a bug in the earlier versions of TCPMAN in the creation of the INI file. For reasons best known to itself, it records some Baud rates wrongly. If it does this to you, then no matter how often you try to correct it in the Setup routine, it will continue to get it wrong. The only solution is to edit the INI file with Notepad, and type the correct value in the **slip-baudrate** line.

Figure 6.2 Correcting the Baud rate bug in TRUMPWSK.INI. This may not be necessary on your version — but check just in case.

```
─              Notepad - TRUMPWSK.INI          ▼  ▲
 File   Edit   Search   Help
[Trumpet Winsock]
ip       = 193.119.97.209
netmask  = 255.255.0.0
gateway  = 0.0.0.0
dns      = 193.119.96.16
time     =
domain   =
vector   = 00
mtu      = 254
rwin     = 1024
mss      = 214
slip-enabled    = 1
slip-port       = 2
slip-baudrate   = 19200
slip-handshake  = 1
slip-compressed = 1
dial-option     = 0
online-check    = 0
inactivity-timeout = 10
slip-timeout    = 10
```

The Login script

A login script is not essential, but without it you will have to type the phone number, your username and password every time you dial in.

Your service provider may have supplied you with a standard LOGIN.CMD script to be edited to include your details. (The *Dialler – Edit Scripts* command in TCPMAN is the simplest way to handle this.) If they haven't, use Notepad to create a script in one of these formats:

Format 1 – with an IP address

output atz\13	(Resets the modem)
input 30 OK	(Waits for an OK from the modem)
output atdt*TEL_NO*\13	(Dials the service)
input 30 CONNECT	(Waits for call to get through)
input 30 ogin:	(Waits for the login: prompt)
output *USERNAME*-slip\13	(Sends your username and connection mode - SLIP or PPP)
input 30 word:	(Waits for the password: prompt)
output *PASSWORD*\13	(Sends your password)
input 30 enabled	(Waits for recognition)

Format 2 – IP address dynamically allocated

output atz\13	(Resets the modem)
input 30 OK	(Waits for an OK from the modem)
output atdt*TEL_NO*\13	(Dials the service)
input 30 CONNECT	(Waits for call to get through)
input 30 ogin:	(Waits for the login: prompt)
output *USERNAME*\13	(Sends your username)
input 30 word:	(Waits for the password: prompt)
output *PASSWORD*\13	(Sends your password)
input 30 otocol:	(Waits for the protocol: prompt)

output slip\13   (Selects SLIP)

input 30 ddress: (Collects the IP address)

address 30

display \n

display Connected. Your IP address for this session is \i. \n

Notes:

● Each output line ends in \13, equivalent to pressing [Enter].
● Don't include the (bracketed) comments.
● Replace the ITALICS with your details.
● Only include the last few characters of the prompts.

To test the script, run TCPMAN and give the *Dialler – Login* command. It will be obvious if it works, as you will get a welcome message or other indication of a successful connection. If

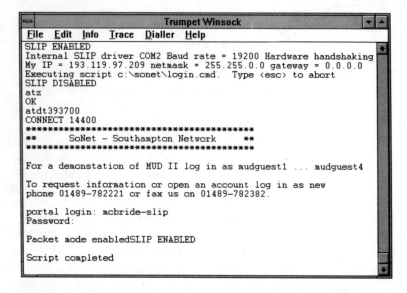

```
SLIP ENABLED
Internal SLIP driver COM2 Baud rate = 19200 Hardware handshaking
My IP = 193.119.97.209 netmask = 255.255.0.0 gateway = 0.0.0.0
Executing script c:\sonet\login.cmd.  Type <esc> to abort
SLIP DISABLED
atz
OK
atdt393700
CONNECT 14400
***********************************************
**       SoNet - Southampton Network        **
***********************************************

For a demonstation of MUD II log in as mudguest1 ... mudguest4

To request information or open an account log in as new
phone 01489-782221 or fax us on 01489-782382.

portal login: mcbride-slip
Password:

Packet mode enabledSLIP ENABLED

Script completed
```

Figure 6.3 Establishing a successful Winsock connection – this time to Sonet. If this was just a test, the next job would be to close the connection with Dialler – Bye.

you do not get through, that does not necessarily show that the script is at fault. You may have made a mistake when setting the TCPMAN configuration; or it may simply be that the lines to the service are busy. Try several times and check your *File – Setup* entries before ringing the service provider for help. (My experience of technical support staff has been that they are a very helpful bunch, who can quickly solve the problem, but that you can be a long time on the phone trying to get hold of them.)

——— 6.4 Using Winsock ———

Once you have got Winsock set up properly, using it is straight-forward, though there are a couple of points that you must watch out for. The normal usage should be:

1 Run TCPMAN from Program Manager.
2 Use *Dialler – Login* to connect to your service.
3 When you have established the connection, minimise the TCPMAN window out of the way and run your **Winsock client** (6.5) application.
4 After you have exited from the client application, restore TCPMAN and use *Dialler – Bye* to close the connection.
5 Use *File – Exit* to shut down TCPMAN.

● If at (2) you cannot get through to your service, because it is busy or off-line, press [Escape] to abort the login script and get the SLIP ENABLED message. (You may need to press it twice.) Check that you have the dialling tone from your phone before trying to login again. TCPMAN does not always release the phone properly. If you can hear the whistle and crackle of a data connection, press the reset button on your modem to clear the line.

● You may have to press [Escape] before TCPMAN will let you exit. Check for the dialling tone after exiting and reset the modem if necessary.

—— 6.5 Winsock clients ——

Winsock, as we saw earlier, simply handles your end of the SLIP/PPP connection, but it does not give you any way of actually doing anything on the Internet. For this, you need client applications. Your service provider should have sent you, or shown you how to download, a set of these – at the very least you should have a Web browser, and with that you can get the rest off the Web. The ones described in this book are all either shareware or freeware.

These client applications should be installed on to your hard disk and all need some configuration before they can be used.

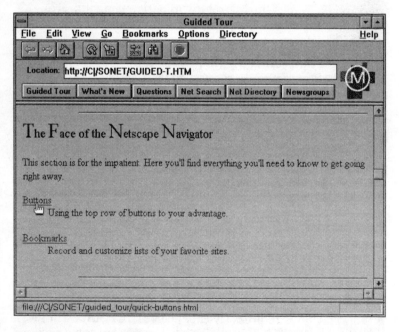

Figure 6.4 Netscape, shown here at the start of its guided tour. The hypertext links, that take you to other pages, are underlined. When the cursor is over one of these, it turns into a hand.

6.6 Eudora

Eudora is typical of the current crop of e-mail packages, and can be used on- or off-line. Before you can use it, you must give it your e-mail address and 'post office' details.

Each time you run Eudora, you will have to supply your password. If you are the only person who uses your computer, this can be an irritant, but if others have access to the machine, you may appreciate being able to keep your mail confidential.

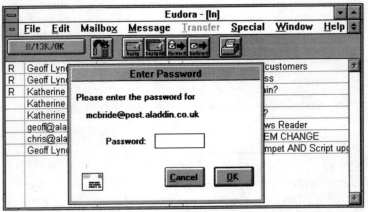

Figure 6.5 You cannot start Eudora without giving the password – your service provider should have set one, though this can be changed once you are in.

There are two aspects to setting up Eudora, both of which are reached through the *Special* menu.

The first, and the only one that is essential, is *Configuration*. Select this to open the Configuration panel, then dig out the documentation that your service provider sent.

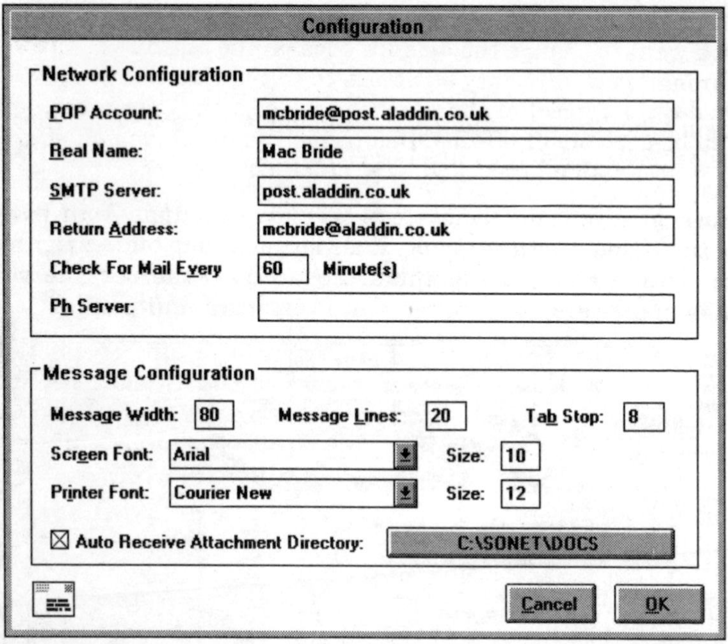

Figure 6.6 Configuring Eudora. Your service provider will supply the details.

Note that there are two addresses – the *Return Address* is your **e-mail address** (7.3) and is the one that other people will use when writing to you; the *POP address* is needed by the e-mail system to identify your Point of Presence connection. The first part of this will be the same as your return address, while the second part should be the same as the *SMTP Server*. If you do not have the details of any of these, get in touch with your service.

The *Check for Mail* every value is irrelevant for most people. It is designed for those users who will be on-line for hours at a time and expect to get mail regularly. For most of us, it is enough to dial in and collect the mail once a day.

In the *Message Configuration* section, select the fonts you want to use on screen and printouts. Eudora allows binary files to be attached to messages, and detached from incoming mail. The

Attachments Directory specifies where these files are stored. If you want to change the default, click on the button and browse through your directory structure to select a new location.

Using the *Special – Switches* command opens the panel shown below. These settings are largely a matter of choice, and you may well want to come back to this when you have had more experience of using the system. Do make sure that *Word Wrap* is turned on, to prevent long lines disappearing off the right of the screen, and make sure that *Leave Mail On Server* is turned off – many providers charge rent for storing your mail!

Turn on *Keep Copies* only if you want to retain copies of all your mail. When you delete messages in Eudora, they are first transferred to a Trash directory. Turning on *Empty Trash On Quit* will stop this from filling up. Leave *Signature?* off until you have designed your **e-mail signature** (9.3).

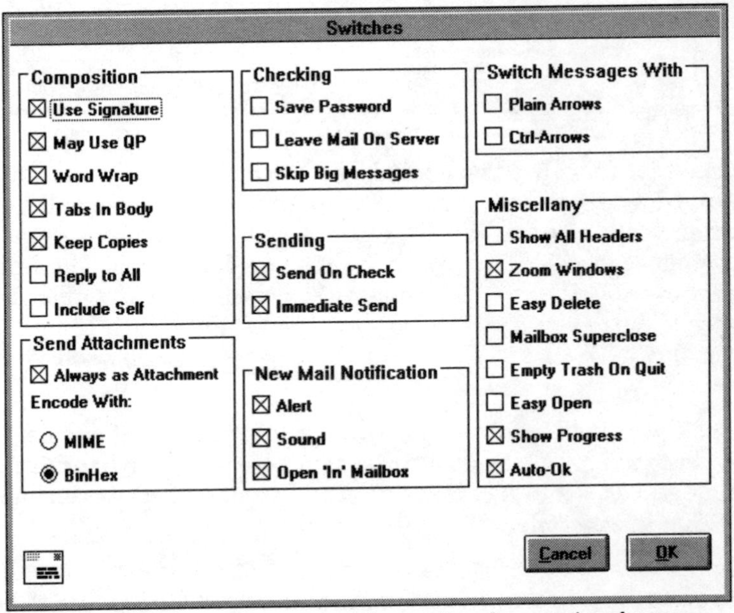

Figure 6.7 Eudroa's Switches are mainly a matter of personal preference.

6.7 Netscape

At the time of writing, this is the Web browser that you are most likely to be offered by a service provider, and is the one to get if you are finding your own applications. Its current version is easier to use and more efficient than the main alternative browser, Mosaic, or the earlier and cruder Cello.

Netscape requires a little configuration before you use it for the first time. All setting up is done from the *Options – Preferences* command, which leads to a set of five panels. You can move between these by selecting from the drop down list at the top.

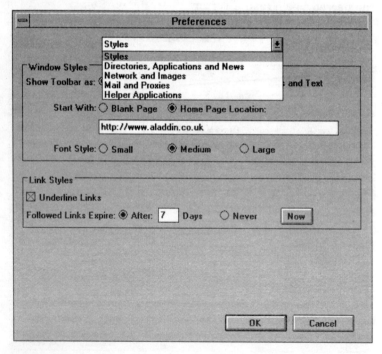

Figure 6.8 Setting the Style preferences in Netscape. Note the drop down list at the top, from which the other preferences panels are reached.

The Styles panel determines the basic screen display. Much of this is simply a matter of choice, but you would probably want to set it to *Start with* your *Home Page Location* – this will be the top level page of your service provider. Click the mouse to locate the cursor in the slot and type in the URL. Your provider should give you this, and it should follow this style:

http://www.aladdin.co.uk

The second Preferences panel that needs attention is *Mail and Proxies*. Here you should type the *Mail Server*, *Your Name*, *Your E-mail* address and site addresses for the *FTP* and *HTTP* (World Wide Web) *Proxy*, plus the *Gopher* and other proxies if you will be using them. Your service provider should supply the necessary details.

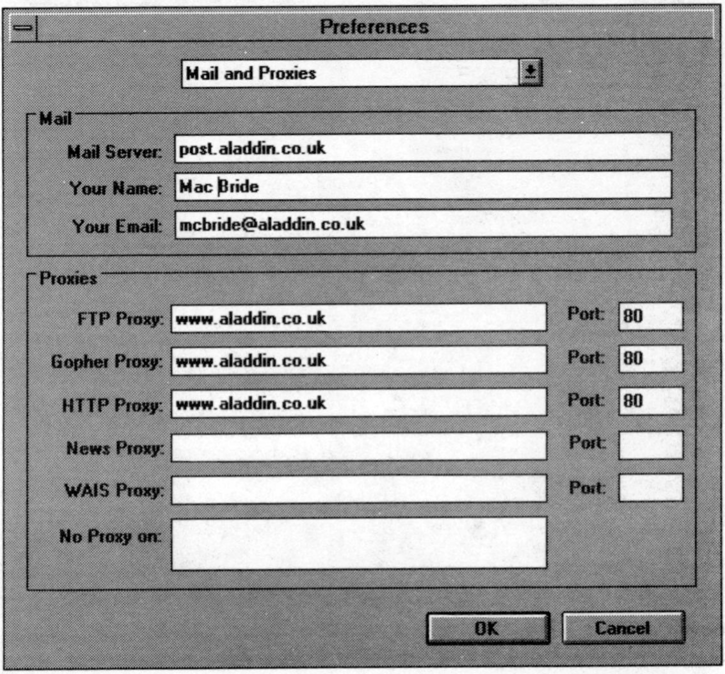

Figure 6.9 The Mail and Proxies Preferences in Netscape. Point and click to locate the text cursor in a slot to enter details.

The final essential setting is in the *Directories, Applications and News* panel, where you should tell Netscape which directory to use for Temporary storage.

You may want to add **helper applications** (8.7) at this point. These are programs that can be linked to Netscape to view graphics or videos or listen to sound files. They can be added at any time, and it might be better to leave this until you have got further into the Web. You will then have a better idea of what is useful – and where and how to find the various viewing tools.

With Eudora and Netscape configured, you now have enough to get started exploring **e-mail** (Section 7) and the **World Wide Web** (Section 8). Jump on to those if you cannot wait any longer!

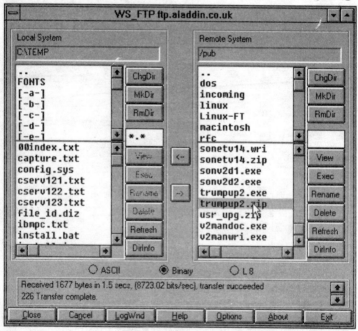

Figure 6.10 One of the alternative layouts for WS_FTP – the local and remote directories can be arranged horizontally, with the commands buttons above or below. The two-line slot at the bottom records your interaction with the remote system. The arrows let you scroll back over this to track down errors.

6.8 WS_FTP

As with Netscape, the configuration options in WS_FTP are a mixture of personal preferences over the screen display, and those settings that are essential for on-line work.

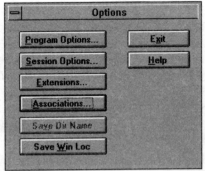

Start by clicking the *Options* button to open the panel shown here.

In the *Program Options* panel, you must enter your *E-mail Address*. This will be needed whenever you connect to a system that uses anonymous **ftp** (11.2) – as most do.

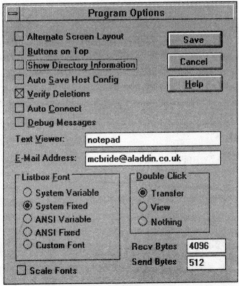

Figure 6.11 The Program Options panel of WS_FTP – apart from the E-mail Address, these can be set to suit yourself.

The *Text Viewer* is used when you try to read the README and Index files on remote computers. You should also select either Notepad or Write or another simple editor/word-processor that can be opened quickly and uses little memory.

When you start to use WS_FTP in earnest, you will find that it offers you the choice of viewing or downloading any chosen file from the remote computer. A neat option here is the way that you can determine the effect of a *Double-Click*. Do you want it to start a file transfer, view a file or do nothing? The *Nothing* option is not as pointless as it seems. If you are a little heavy-handed with the mouse, it is all too easy to start downloading or viewing a file that you really have no interest in!

Leave the *Receive* and *Send Bytes* figures at their defaults.

The other *Program Options* are largely a matter of personal preference. Try the *alternative screen layouts* and *button* placements to see which you like.

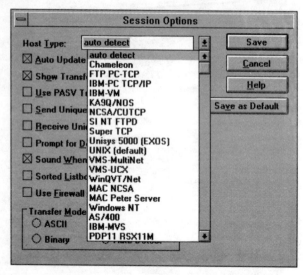

Figure 6.12 In Session Options, select auto-detect for Host Type and Transfer Mode and save yourself bother!

On the *Session Options* panel, you should make sure that the *Host Type* is set to *auto-detect* – pull down the list and select it if necessary. One look at the length and complexity of that list should be enough to convince you that this is best left to the system! The *Transfer Mode* is likewise best set to *auto-detect*. It will then transfer binary and text files in the appropriate manner, without you having to select the mode each time.

When looking at *Program Options*, we noted that WS_FTP lets you to view files on a remote computer. If they are text files, they will be handled by the Text Viewer, but what if they are other types? This is where the *Associate* options come into play. They allow you to specify which programs to use to view different types of files, just as Windows allows you to associate certain file types with certain programs.

The associations are set up in the same way. Pull down the *Files with Extension* list and select an extension. It will try to find the appropriate *Associate With* program, but if nothing appears in that slot, select the program from the list below, or use the *Browse* button to search elsewhere on your system.

At this initial stage, it is probably worth running through the extension list and picking up those assossiations that come automatically, but leaving others until later. Until you start to ftp, it is difficult to forecast which types of files you will actually want to view.

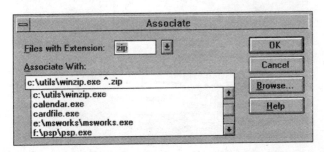

Figure 6.13 Setting up an Association for a file type may require no more than selecting its extension from the drop-down list.

6.9 HGopher

Hgopher is a good example of Gopher Plus software. Being Gopher Plus means that it can cope with a wide variety of file types and get the best out of the Internet's Gopher system. **Setting up viewers** (12.3), not just to handle different types, but to handle them in the most efficient manner, is an art and takes a while to do. At this stage, it is probably best to ignore them and just do the minimum that is necessary to get started with the Gopher system.

Configuration is done through the *Options* menu, and two sections need attention – *Gopher Set Up* and *Network Set Up*.

Viewer, *Language* and *Server Set Up* are all interrelated and are best left until later.

Fonts can be changed to suit yourself at any time.

Options
Flush Cache
Copy Mode ▶
Gopher Set Up...
Network Set Up...
V**i**ewer Set up...
Language Set up...
Server Set up...
Gopher Fl**a**gs...
F**o**nts...

Start by selecting *Options – Network Set Up*. With a dial up SLIP/PPP connection, all you should do here is make sure that the *Use Vendor provided* check box is on and *Use DNS* is off. The *DNS Setup* slots can all be left blank.

Figure 6.14 in HGopher's Network Setup, the details of the DNS Setup are only required with a few unusual systems.

As the Gopher system is menu-driven, you need to get into a menu to start the process. This start point is defined in the *Gopher Server* slot of the *Gopher Set Up* panel. Check out the list of **Gopher Servers** (14.5) to find one that is near to you – there is no point in going further than is necessary. Simply type the site name into the top slot; set the *Port* number to 70 and leave the *Selector* blank, so that you go in at the top level menu.

HGopher creates temporary files while it is running and deletes them on exit. The *Tmp Directory* is where these will be stored. This may as well be the same directory that is used for temporary storage by other Windows programs. It is worth setting up a separate, new *Save To Directory* for any files that you download while running gopher.

The rest of the settings can be left at their defaults for now.

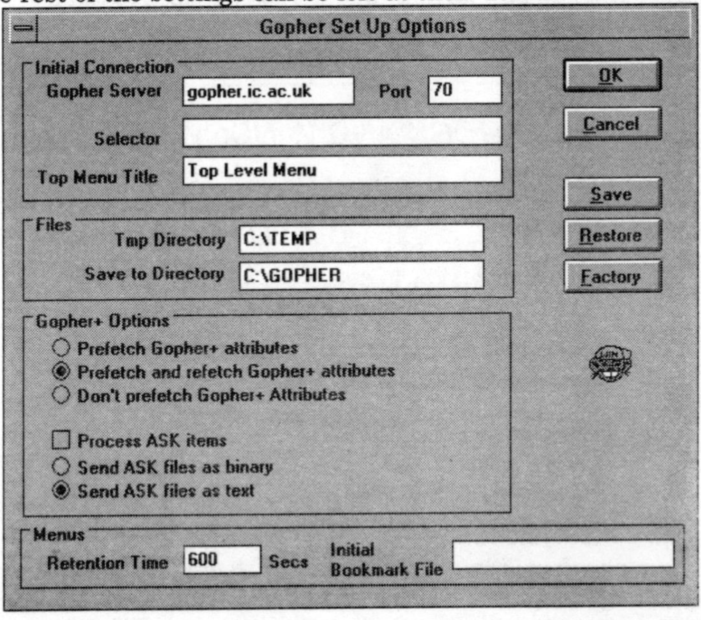

Figure 6.15   With this set up, the first connection to the Gopher system will be at Imperial College, London (gopher.ic.ac.uk).

6.10 Summary

- The SLIP and PPP protocols allow computers to transfer data as easily over the Internet as they could over a small office network.

- You need Trumpet Winsock to handle your end of a SLIP or PPP connection to get interactive access to the Internet.

- The TCPMAN program and the Login script must be configured before you can use Winsock.

- To do anything over a Winsock link, you need client applications programs.

- Netscape, a Web browser, is probably the most widely used of all Winsock clients, others include Eudora mail software, WS_FTP for file transfer and HGopher to handle travels around the Gopher information system.

WINSOCK AND WINDOWS 95

Windows 95 has its own Winsock, part of the Dial-Up Networking software. You can use this, but connections can be extremely fiddly to set up – unless your service provider can give you detailed advice, don't try.

The standard Trumpet Winsock works perfectly well, once it is installed successfully – and there is a trick to this. Windows 95 treats its own version of Winsock as essential, and automatically replaces any WINSOCK.DLL in the \Windows\System folder with this. So, immediately after installing Winsock, move the new WINSOCK.DLL from the \Windows\System folder into the folder containing your Internet applications. It will work just as well from there, and it will be safe from Windows 95!

7

ELECTRONIC MAIL

——— 7.1 Aims of this chapter ———

E-mail is the simplest of all the Internet activities. It is based on **ASCII files** (3.3), i.e. plain text, and can be managed by a basic communications program, such as **Terminal** (5.3), though it is more conveniently handled by special mail software. This simplicity in no way detracts from its value – some people find it the most useful of all the Internet's facilities. In this chapter we look at the practicalities of sending and receiving e-mail, dip into the conventions of electronic communications and explore some typical e-mail software.

HOW DOES THE MAIL GET THROUGH?

After a message is sent to your service provider, it may pass through a dozen computers before reaching its destination. At each it is held briefly, while the computer assembles a handful of messages to send to the next place. At the cost of a slight delay, this gives more efficient Internet traffic.

—— 7.2 Ups and Downs of E-mail ——

E-mail has several advantages – and a few disadvantages – compared to ordinary mail. Bear these in mind when deciding which to use.

● Delivery is fast, from as little as half an hour up to a maximum of a day.
● It's very cheap to use, costing only a few seconds of phone time, and possibly on-line charges, whether you are sending it overseas or down the road.
● You can send multiple copies as easily as you can send one.
● Incoming mail can be easily annotated and returned to its sender, or forwarded to other people.

And the disadvantages..

● E-mail does not always get through. The slightest error in the address is enough to prevent a delivery, and even when you do everything right, there is always the chance of a failure in one of the links between you and your recipient.
● Not everyone checks their e-mail regularly, while an envelope on the mat by the front door will get read.

—— 7.3 Addresses for mailing ——

Before you can write to anyone, you must know their address. Now, while addresses follow simple rules and are fairly easy to remember, you cannot work them out for yourself and you must get them exactly right. The basic pattern is:

name@site.address

Notice the punctuation – an @ sign after the name, and dots between the constituent parts of the site address.

The **name** is usually based on the user's real name, though how it is formed varies between organisations. 'Johnny B. Goode', for example, might be allocated the names 'jbgoode', 'johnnyg', 'John_Goode', 'johnny.b.goode', 'goode3' or other variations. Notice that both _ and . are used for punctuation, and that sometimes a number will be added, especially to common names. Some organisations ignore the person's real name completely and allocate numbers or special user names.

The **site addresses** are often the same as those of the organisation to which the user belongs, though some service providers allocate a separate domain name to each of their members.

The following examples are of names that have been allocated to me while I have been trying out different service providers:

mcbride@aladdin.co.uk

macbride1@delphi.com

macbride@macdesign.win-uk.net

100407.2521@compuserve.com

You will see that between them these cover many of the variations noted above. One address that does need special attention is that for CompuServe. When logging in to the system, the name is written with a comma for punctuation – '100407,2521' – but when used as part of an e-mail address, the comma is replaced by a dot – '100407.2521'. These little things were meant to try us!

Finding addresses

If you are a member of CompuServe, it is easy enough to find the e-mail address of any other CompuServe member – there is a directory that you can search by name/town/country. Some other services also offer similar facilities for finding members of the same service, and large organisations normally have internal directories. Some of these directories can be searched by 'outsiders' using WHOIS or other people-finding programs, but just as the Internet is not a single organisation, so there is no single directory that holds the addresses of Internet users.

The simplest way to get someone's address is to ask them – but don't ask them to tell you over the phone, for people make mistakes (especially as they do not normally write to themselves). Instead, ask them to send e-mail to you. When the message comes in it will have their address at the top, and you can be confident that it is exactly right.

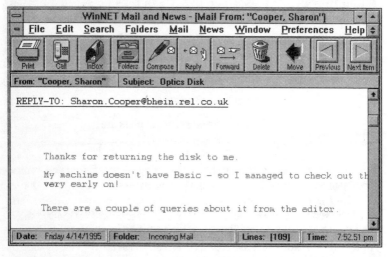

Figure 7.1 In the WinNet Mail system, the sender's address is clearly visible in the REPLY TO: line.

7.4 Sending mail

All e-mail software handles the mail in much the same way. You start with a *Compose mail* or *Create mail* command, and this will take you into an editor. There you will be presented with three slots, normally headed To:, CC: and Subject:.

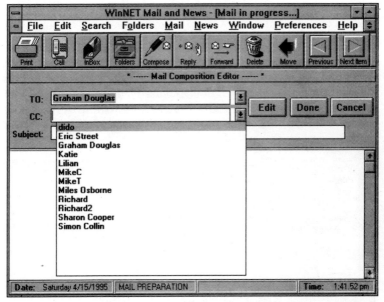

Figure 7.2 In WinNET mail, as in other good mail software, you can record your contacts in an address book and select them by name. The system will translate the names into e-mail addresses before sending the mail.

- **To:** as you would expect, is the address of the recipient.
- **CC:** is for the addresses of those people, if any, to whom you want to send copies.
- **Subject:** should have a few words outlining the nature of your message. You will see why in a moment.

To create the message itself, you have three choices.

- If you can get on with the mail's own editor, then move your cursor into the message area and type it directly.
- If you prefer to work in your favourite word-processor, then you could create the message there and use Window's Cut and Paste facility to transfer it into the mail editor.
- The third alternative is to use your word-processor and save the message as an ASCII text file. This can then be imported into your mail.

If you are a poor typist or an indifferent speller, one or other of the methods that uses a word-processor will be best, as you can run your text through its spell checker. You will be surprised at the number of typing errors that you find in people's e-mail.

When you have finished, you can send the message immediately, if you are on-line already, or store it for sending later when you go on-line.

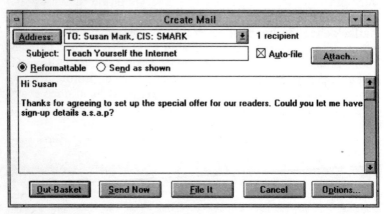

Figure 7.3 CompuServe's Create Mail routine offers the choice of storing mail in the Out-basket for later delivery or sending mail immediately – and it will dial up for you if you are not already on-line.

On-line and Off-line

Remember that you do not need to be connected to your service provider to read or write messages. In general, it is simplest to write or to read and reply to short messages while you are on-line, but to handle longer texts off-line.

7.5 Incoming mail

It may be obvious, but it is worth stating that e-mail does not get delivered directly to you. Instead, it goes into a mailbox at your service provider and you must log in to get it. (This is not true if you are on a network in an organisation, where the network manager will collect mail for everyone and distribute it.) Some services will automatically delete your mail from the mailbox once you have collected a copy; others will give you the option of leaving it there or deleting it. Opt to have it deleted. There is no point in retaining copies elsewhere, and they will probably charge you for storage beyond a bare minimum. Checking and emptying your mailbox regularly – at least once every couple of days – will also keep your service happy and your charges down.

R	Geoff Lynch	17:57 06/12/94 C	2	Reward for existing customers
	Katherine Chaffe	09:21 07/02/95 -(	2	Re: Arizona
	Katherine Chaffe	11:21 27/03/95 -(	3	Re: Michael visiting?
	geoff@aladdin.cc	00:06 28/03/95	1	Offline Windows News Reader
	chris@aladdin.cc	09:22 04/04/95	3	IMPORTANT SYSTEM CHANGE
	Geoff Lynch	22:40 12/04/95	3	Later Version of Trumpet AND Script upgrad

Figure 7.4 The In-tray of Eudora mail. As you can see, it can also serve as a storage area for old mail.

New mail will normally be placed into an 'In-tray', where it will appear as a single line entry showing the sender, the date and whatever the sender wrote in their Subject line. After looking at the sender and the subject, you can decide whether you want to read it immediately, later or not at all. (There is a certain amount of junk mail that can find its way into your box.) If you store messages for long-term reference, those subject lines will help to identify them.

Double-clicking on a message will open an editor, where you can read the text. It is in an editor, rather than just a viewer, as you may want to use the message actively. Any good e-mail software will give you several options for dealing with mail. You should be able to:

● **reply**, including the original text, if desired. There is usually a facility for editing that text, to cut out unwanted material and add comments.
● **forward** the mail to someone else, perhaps after editing.
● **save** the message as a plain text file.
● **copy or cut** part of the message, pasting it into a word-processed file, using the standard Windows Edit routines.
● **delete** the message.

—————— 7.6 Mail etiquette ——————

Where you are writing to people you know well, there are only a couple of rules of etiquette that you should observe – apart from those same niceties that apply to any form of mail.

● Try to keep your e-mail messages short and to the point. Most of us pay for phone time, and many of us pay for on-line time as we download the mail. It's not nice to run up other people's phone bills! Of course, if you are on-line as you write, short messages will also keep your costs down.
● Annotating and forwarding e-mail is very easy to do, but remember that other people's mail is their copyright, so don't forward without their permission.

If you will be writing to comparative strangers, following the **Newsgroup Netiquette** (9.4) conventions can help to keep communications smooth.

7.7 CompuServe mail

If you join CompuServe and use their WinCIM (or DosCIM) Information Manager package, you will have good, easy-to-use e-mail facilities. These include a simple but effective editor, three ready-made storage areas – an *In-Basket*, *Out-Basket* and *Filing Cabinet* – and a *Send File* command for sending text you have composed on a word-processor. Binary files can also be attached to mail and transmitted through *Send File*.

The commands are accessed from the Mail menu, with some duplicated by icons on the ribbon at the top of the screen.

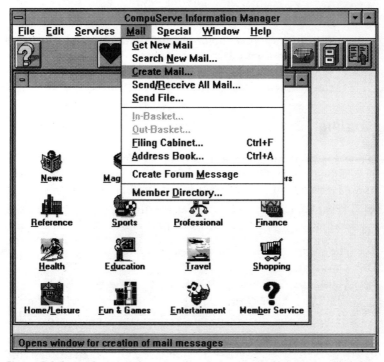

Figure 7.5 CompuServe's Information Manager, with the Mail menu pulled down to show the range of facilities.

The *Get New Mail* icon is only present when you are on-line. It checks your mailbox and retrieves any messages. Oddly, the equivalent menu command is available off-line, and if used then will dial-in to collect the mail.

 The *In-Basket* command and icon are active when new mail has been received and has not yet been deleted or stored elsewhere.

 The *Out-Basket* command and icon are active when you have created new mail and stored it for later sending. If wanted, you can edit or delete these messages.

 The *Filing Cabinet* is where old mail can be stored. It has two ready-made folders, and new ones can be created if you want to keep your files neatly organised.

 The *Address Book* holds the names and e-mail addresses of your contacts. Its presence means that you only have to type a person's e-mail address correctly once – after that you can select them by name from the book.

Sending mail

A new message normally starts with the *Create Mail* command. This takes you first to the *Recipient List* where you select the names of those to whom the message will be sent.

Notice the radio buttons at the top left, that identify the category of recipient. There are *three* options:

To: the main, and perhaps the only, recipient
CC: those who get normal copies
BC: those who get **B**lind **C**opies – ones not showing the distribution list. This is not found on all e-mail software.

E-mail addresses can either be selected from the *Address Book* and copied into the *Recipients* with `Copy »` or typed directly into the *Address* slot. When they are sorted out, `OK` takes you to the editor (Figure 7.3) to write your message. Mail can be sent immediately or stored in the Out-Basket.

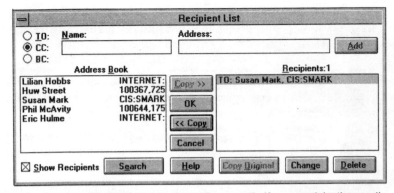

Figure 7.6 The Recipient List in CompuServe mail. If your recipient's e-mail address is not in your book, it can be added at this point.

Collecting mail

A key point to note about collecting mail is that retrieving it from your mailbox does not automatically delete the copies that are stored there – and there is a limit to how much you can store free of charge. As there are very few situations in which you would not want to delete retrieved mail, the simplest solution is to opt for automatic deletion in the Mail Preferences (open the panel with the *Special – Preferences – Mail* command).

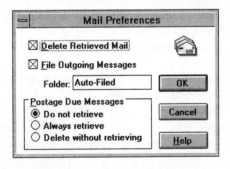

Figure 7.7 Check the Delete Retrieved Mail option in the Mail Preferences, and the File Outgoing Messages option, if you want to keep copies of the mail that you send.

Incoming mail is stored in the In-Basket. Opening a message there takes you into a viewing window, with the Subject line forming its title.

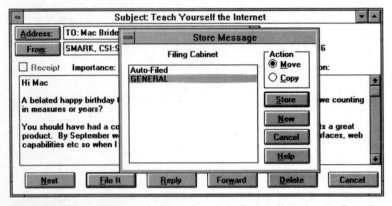

Figure 7.8 Filing a message in CompuServe's In-Basket. Note that the From line includes the sender's name and e-mail address.

You have several ways of dealing with messages.

Next simply leaves the message in the In-basket, and pulls up the next message for viewing.

File It opens the Store Message panel. Incoming messages are normally stored in the GENERAL folder; Auto-Filed is where copies of outgoing messages are kept. Note that Moving a message removes it from the In-Basket, but Copy leaves a copy there as well.

Reply takes you into the editor, without copying the original message. If you want to include it, use the *Edit – Copy* and *Edit – Paste* commands.

Forward also takes you to the editor (via the Recipient List panel), but this time copies the original message, complete with its sender, recipient and date details.

Delete removes the message from the In-Basket.

Cancel exits from the viewer without doing anything to the message.

Files by E-mail

The *Mail – Send File* command allows you to send graphics, programs, data files and plain or formatted text files from a word-processor through the e-mail system. WinCIM does all the hard work for you, but make a note of the directory path and name of the file before you start, as there is no means to browse through directories to find a file within the Send File routine.

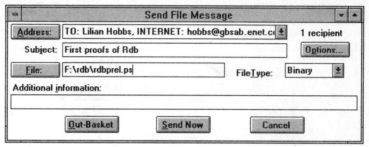

Figure 7.9 The Send File Message panel. You must have the file specifications at hand when you start this.

Off-line work

There is a special facility for those times when you just want to use CompuServe to get up to date with your e-mail. The *Send / Receive All Mail* command will clear your Out-Basket and download any waiting mail into the In-Basket – deleting them from your mailbox automatically. When you give it, you will see this panel:

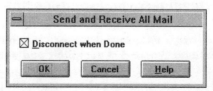

Make sure that the *Disconnect when Done* option is selected, unless you want to stay on-line to use other services.

As you can send and receive a dozen mail message in a minute or so, preparing and reading your mail off-line can dramatically reduce your phone bills and connection charges.

The Member Directory

If you want to write to another CompuServe member, but do not know their address, you can look it up easily in the *Member Directory*. Use this option on the *Mail* menu and type what you know about the person in the Search form. When you start the search, WinCIM dials into CompuServe and checks the directory for you.

Figure 7.10 Setting up a search in the Member Directory. The more details you give, the better, but it will work on partial names if necessary.

You may find it worth trying the Directory for long-lost friends. As CompuServe has nearly 3 million members, there is a reasonable chance that some will be in there.

Mailing to members and non-members

To write to another CompuServe member, all you need is their membership number, as this is also their address. But remember that feature we noted earlier when looking at **addresses for mailing** (7.3) – the comma in the membership number gets changed to a dot in the address. e.g.

Membership No: 100407,2521

becomes:

E-mail address: 100407.2521

To write to someone outside the CompuServe system, you must preface their address with **INTERNET:** e.g.

INTERNET:macbride@macdesign.win-uk.net

Note the punctuation, colon before the address, and no spaces.

If people want to e-mail to you from outside CompuServe, your address is your number followed by @compuserve.com. e.g.

100407.2521@compuserve.com

7.8 WinNet Mail

WinNET Mail and News service is run by the PC User Group. There are two key features to this service – it is designed for purely off-line work and it gives access to e-mail and **newsgroups** (Section 9). If you want an interactive SLIP connection to the Internet, the PC User Group also offers that, but through its CONNECT service.

When you join WinNET Mail you will be supplied with two packages – the main e-mail software, and WinNET Tools, a set of utilities that handle newsgroup subscription, the storage of news articles, the mail queue, and other facilities.

The Call Server

Call Server

This manages your connection to WinNET. When you run this program, it dials into the service, sends any mail you have prepared and downloads incoming mail and newsgroup articles. It then closes down the connection and starts the Mail Manager software that sorts the new files for you.

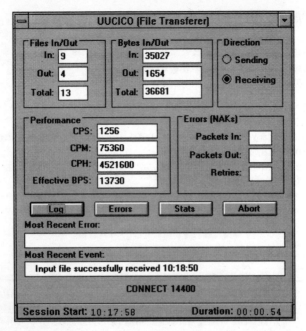

Figure 7.11 The Call Server in action. The title UUCICO stands for Unix to Unix Copy In, Copy Out.

The Call Server can be minimised and run in the background while you do other things, but it is sometimes useful to watch the progress of your connection. The *Performance* figures show you how fast data is being transferred. They will fluctuate but should stay around the nominal level for your connection. For example, if you were running at 14400 Baud, the *Effective BPS* should not drop much below 12000. If it does, you've got a poor connection, and it might be an idea to abort the session and try again later.

This is a very efficient and economical system. If you are sending and receiving only a few e-mail messages a day, and have subscribed to a couple of newsgroups, you should find that your on-line time is not much more than one minute a day.

The Mail and News Software

WinNET Mail and News

This has a comprehensive set of commands on its menus, while the icons duplicate the main e-mail functions and other commonly-used commands.

Compose takes you into the editor, which gives access to the address book (Figures 7.1 and 7.2).

Reply offers you the option of copying in the original message before starting the editor.

Forward automatically copies in the message, adding a FORWARDED TO... header.

Move transfers the message into another folder – a Copy option is also available on the Mail menu.

Call runs the Call Server, if you want to send your new mail immediately.

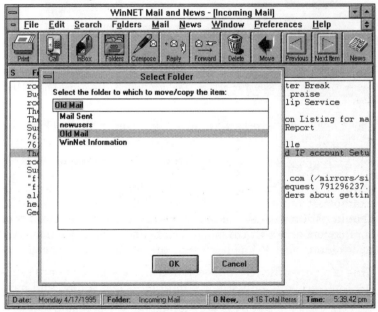

Figure 7.12 WinNET Mail in the middle of moving a file into storage in the Old Mail folder. Simplicity and clarity is a key feature of this software.

The Tools

Some of these duplicate access to programs that can be run directly from Program Manager, but having them all at hand is a convenience. Others can only be accessed via Tools buttons.

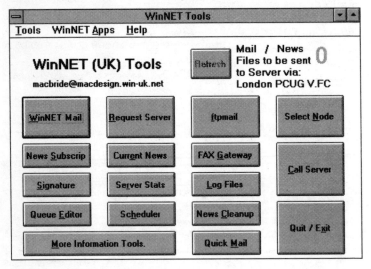

Figure 7.13 WinNET Tools. In the current version the More Information Tools button is merely a promise of things to come, but the others all work!

Those that are news-related will be dealt with later when we look at **newsgroups** (Section 9), and **ftpmail** is covered under **ftp by mail** (11.7). Three that are worth noting here.

Queue Editor takes you to the mail queue – the equivalent of CompuServe's Out-Basket. You cannot actually edit a message once it has been sent there, but you can delete items.

Fax Gateway allows you to send faxes from your computer, through the e-mail system. Even if you have a fax built into your modem, this may be useful, if the phone call to your recipient would be more than that to WinNET.

Quick Mail is intended for sending binary or prewritten text files by mail. It takes you to a panel that collects the e-mail address and subject details, and leads to the *Attach* panel. This lets you browse through your directories to find files. When you select a file, it is converted into **7-bit ASCII** (3.3) before being attached to the message.

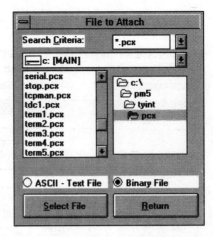

_____ **7.9 Binary files by mail** _____

Binary files can also be attached to messages composed in the normal mail editor, and they can be detached from incoming mail. This is very easy to do – it is just a matter of giving the *Attach binary file* or *Detach binary file* commands, and leaving the rest to the software. An attached file just gets stuck on to the end of your message; a detached file appears in your WinNET directory. But there are a couple of catches ..

E-mail messages are normally restricted to a maximum of around 1,000 lines. A large program or a large image file could well convert to far more than that. If you want to send a large file, you have to chop it up over several messages; and files that arrive in a number of pieces must be stitched back together in an editor, then decoded.

WinNET Mail converts binary files to and from ASCII format with two program called uuencode and uudecode. This are in common use in the Unix world, which includes the **newsgroups** (Section 9), so it is fine for any graphics or other files that you

```
Hi Graham

Here's that logo you wanted, in PCX format.

begin 640 TY.PCX
M"@4!"      !+ %%L ( -8 D<$  ">"\@_P'"6:[=>>R#_/,,3)OP'#R:PX/[SDT
M;,\Q    , ,@_,F_  <+841P2N N !3        0#(:P  KQ P?Q_P  S&L$$%%9\3
M,F_.::SL)  "N S)O 0"?$_5K^@L7"         ,F\!#! Y#( 0 !  \Q<@?? ___\W____-
M____S?___\W____-____S?___\W____-____S?___\W____-
____S?___\W_
MWO&_  .C_WO&_  .C_W?_!^^  8  Z/_=_\<  Z/_+_  @  R?_+_  @  R?_+_  @
R?_+
M_\0  S?_&  ,'XW/_$  ,G_R__$  ,W_Q@@#=__\0  R?_+_\0  S?_&  -W_Q  #)_\O_
...
...
MP?C"  .3_W/_&  ,/_P@#!!^^.3_V__!^^  8  P?_!^^,,  Y?_;_\L  YO_;_\H  Y__;
M_\D  Z/_;_\@  Z?_<_\'XQ   #K____S?___\W____-____S?___\W____-____
MS?\\     @    (  @(     " @ "   (" P,# P-S I,CP@@/__0("  @/\  0$$
M__^  _X  _X"  @$$  @  #  #(#__  !  0((  !  0   "  R?_$  ___
M                     _OPH#*^"D@@(("  _P_  ^  \_   #__#__
&    /_____
```

end
```

**Figure 7.14** An example of a message containing a uuencoded binary file. If you wanted to decode this yourself, you would cut the text from the *begin* to the *end* lines, inclusive, save that as a file then feed it into uudecode. The binary file's name is written into the *begin* line, and will be used by uudecode.

are transferring through the news system. It also works for transferring files with other people whose e-mail software uses the same conversion system. Unfortunately, not all do. There are several different ways to send binaries by mail, and they are all in use somewhere or other.

# 7.10 Eudora

Eudora mail can be used either on- or off-line, through a Winsock and SLIP/PPP connection. It is comprehensive in its mailing facilities, though not as user-friendly as perhaps it could be.
```

We noticed earlier, when **setting up Eudora** (6.6) that it could be extensively configured to your own liking – it is a shame that there are neither Help pages nor user documentation in the current version.

Most of the mail-handling commands are on the *Message* menu. You may note the presence of a *Redirect* as well as a *Forward* option. The *Delete* option moves files from the *In* and *Out* trays to the *Trash* can. It only removes files from the system if used within the Trash can. This two-stage deletion does ensure that you do not delete messages by mistake.

Message	
New Message	Ctrl+N
Reply	Ctrl+R
Forward	
Redirect	
Send Again	
New Message To	▶
Reply To	▶
Forward To	▶
Redirect To	▶
Send Immediately	Ctrl+E
Change Queueing...	
Attach Document...	Ctrl+H
Delete	Ctrl+D

The address book is hidden on the *Window* menu under *Nicknames*. Once an e-mail address and its nickname have been entered into this, typing a nickname for the recipient will pull in the correct address before mailing.

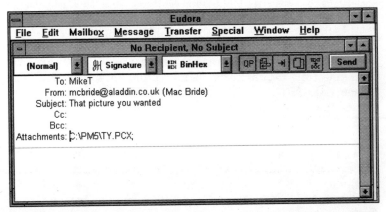

Figure 7.15 Creating a new message in Eudora. The system will replace MikeT in the To: line with his e-mail address from the Nickname list. Notice that Eudora, like CompuServe, has a Blind Copy facility.

Attached files

When you are attaching files in Eudora, you have a choice of two conversion methods, MIME and BinHex. MIME is the Multipurpose Internet Mail Extension, and is in common use on the World Wide Web and other parts of the Internet; BinHex is a simpler encoder along the lines of uuencode. Either will work equally well, but as with binaries sent through WinNET, the most important thing to check is that your recipient can get the binaries out of the mail when it reaches the other end. Send a short test file before trying to mail anything that matters.

7.11 Summary

- Treat e-mail messages as memos rather than letters. Keep them short and to the point, and remember that you can send copies to other people.
- You must know a person's exact e-mail address before you can write to them. The best way to get the address it to ask them to send you mail.
- It is more convenient, and cheaper to read and write mail off-line, so whatever service provider you use, make sure that their software offers this facility.
- If you are a CompuServe member, you only need a person's number to write to other members, but to mail outside the system you need their full address, and must prefix it with INTERNET:.
- WinNET Mail is a specialised service for those who only want e-mail and newsgroup access, and it probably the best way to handle these aspects of the Internet.
- Eudora mail is a comprehensive, but not user-friendly, Winsock client for use on SLIP/PPP connections.
- Most e-mail software offers a means of attaching binary files to messages, but different packages use different conversion methods.

8

THE WORLD WIDE WEB

—— 8.1 Aims of this chapter ——

The World Wide Web links together around four million computers and countless Gigabytes of data. Using **Netscape** (8.3), **Spry Mosaic** (8.11) or any other Web browser, you can access:

- most **newsgroups** (9.8)
- many **ftp sites** (11.6)
- the **Gopher system** (12.4)
- plus the interlined, interactive, informative, in-full-colour pages of the Web itself.

It just is not possible to cover the Web properly in 20 or so pages. The more limited aims of this chapter are to introduce some of the tools, some of the central concepts and some of the entry points. After that, you are on your own! But don't worry. The World Wide Web is the Internet at its friendliest.

If you like abbreviations, the World Wide Web is referred to as WWW (shorter to write, but longer to say), W3 and the Web. Please yourself which – I prefer the last.

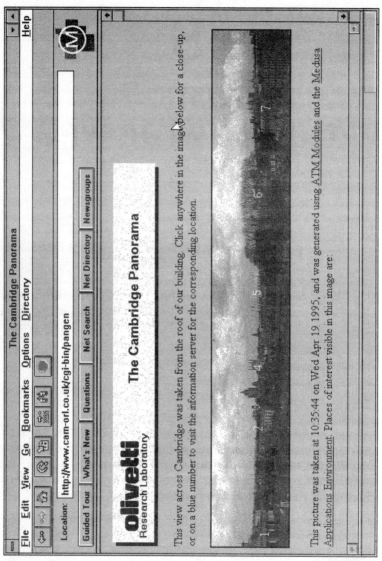

Figure 8.1 Olivetti's Cambridge Panorama. The page has hot links in its picture and hypertext links in its text.

—— 8.2 The Hyperlinked Web ——

The World Wide Web is a collection of linked documents, or **pages**, that span the Internet. The pages are written in **HTML** – HyperText Markup Language (Section 13) which defines the font styles and layout of the pages and, more importantly, creates the links to other documents. These **hyperlinks** appear in the text as an underlined word or phrase, coloured in blue if it has not been used, or in red after the link has been made. Clicking on a hyperlink calls up the linked page, where you will find other links to other pages.

In simple terms, what is happening is this. When the HTML document is written, hyperlink phrases have attached to them the URL of another page. Clicking on the phrase or image makes the Web browser pick up this URL and send it down the line to the remote computer. This makes the connection to whichever computer hosts the linked page, and passes the connection back to you – invisibly and at the click of a button. The links are processed and the documents transferred using HTTP, the HyperText Transfer Protocol. This is why the **URL**s (2.8) of Web pages always start with *http*.

Hyperlinks can also be embedded in a picture or an icon. You will usually be alerted to them by an accompanying caption.

Olivetti Research Laboratory's Cambridge Panorama, shown opposite, is a real-time panoramic view of the city, taken by a camera on Olivetti's rooftop. Its digitised picture is fed back into the Web, and to some extent it can be controlled through the Web. This is a fascinating, if fairly useless, piece of techological wizardry, but it does give an good demonstration the type of links that can be embedded in a Web page.

- Clicking on a number takes you to a page on the server in the numbered building.
- Clicking elsewhere on the picture produces a close up.
- Clicking on the underlined text in the caption takes you to pages that explain more about how it works.

Figure 8.2 A close up of King's College Chapel, from the Cambridge Panorama. This looked better in colour on screen, but the resolution of photographs over the Web is not that high – higher resolution means larger files and slower transfers.

An increasing number of service providers are offering their members the opportunity to set up their own personal Web pages, either free or at low cost. If you are offered this and want to take it up, you will have to learn how to write hypertext. **Using HTML** (13.1) is straightforward enough as long as you don't try to do anything too clever. You will soon pick up enough to be able to create an attractive page.

PAGES AND PICTURES

Many Web pages contain photos or other images, which may be 100k or more. As many are company logos, photos of the page owners and other purely decorative images, and as they take a while to download even over a fast link, it is best to turn off the automatic loading of images when **configuring Netscape** (6.7). Text comes in quickly, and from the text you should be able to tell whether the graphics are worth seeing. If they are, you can load the images later.

8.3 Netscape

At the time of writing, Netscape is the Web browser that most people choose to use – this is partly because the current version is available free, but largely because of its combination of power and simplicity. If you have used other Windows applications, you should have few problems with Netscape.

There is a comprehensive set of commands in its menu system, though in practice there are only a few that you will want to use regularly. These are duplicated by icons. You will use few commands because most of your active work in Netscape will consist of moving between pages by clicking on hypertext links.

 Go – Back to the page you were on before opening the current one;

 Go – Forward to the next open page (can only be used after going back)

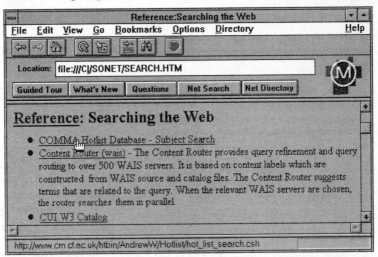

Figure 8.3 Netscape at work. The URL of the current page is shown in the Location slot. Notice that when you point at a hypertext link, the URL of the linked page is displayed in the status line at the bottom.

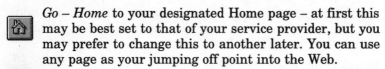

Go – Home to your designated Home page – at first this may be best set to that of your service provider, but you may prefer to change this to another later. You can use any page as your jumping off point into the Web.

View – Reload the current page

View – Load Images, used when automatic loading is turned off and you want to see those on the current page

File – Open Location, used to go straight to a page by giving its **URL** (8.5)

Edit – Find will search through the current page for a word or phrase – very useful given the length of some of the pages that are around

Go – Stop Loading is invaluable for those frequent times when you realise at the start of a long download that you do not really want to see that page.

SAVING PAGES

Note the command *File – Save As*. You can use this to save the current page to disk, to read later when you are off-line. Save pages with the .htm extension and you can reload them into Netscape when you are off-line, using *File – Open File*.

——— 8.4 Net Directories ———

Hypertext and hot links provide an efficient means of following threads from page to page, but with so much information spread over so many pages on so many sites over the Web, the problem is where to start looking. You will normally have the home page of your service provider, and this will have some start points, but not necessarily that many, nor in the direction that you want to go. After you have been exploring the Web for a while you will have your own **bookmarks** (8.6) to get you to key pages – but you have to find them first.

Fortunately, a number of organisations maintain directories and jumping off points. Some of these are focused on specific topics, others offer a systematic overview of the Web's resources.

Yahoo

Yahoo is one of the best of the general directories. It is growing rapidly, both in size and scope. When I first started on this book, a few months ago, it had direct links to just under 30,000 pages. Now it links to around 38,000 pages – many with links to others, and it seems to cover almost every conceivable topic.

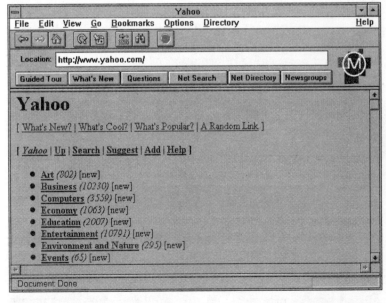

Figure 8.4 The Yahoo Home page with the top level menu of the directory. The page's URL is http://www.yahoo.com.

Apart from the main subject directory, they also offer:

- **What's New** – organised purely by date; while it is interesting to see what's been added to the Web in the last few days, or whenever, this is not a viable route for finding material on any given topic.
- **What's Cool** – a collection of links to intriguing sites, and well worth a visit. Here you will find **Interesting devices connected to the Web**, and pages which are fascinating if only for the amazingly trivial nature of their contents!
- **What's Popular** – another collection of assorted links. Browsing these will give you an idea of the intersts of the average Web user.
- **A Random Link** – which could be to anywhere!

The directory structure is simple and effective. If an item has a number after it, it indicates that it leads to another menu, and the number is how many pages can be reached through that menu, directly or indirectly. [new] at the end of the line indicates that pages have been added within the last few days. You would normally expect to work through two or three levels of menus before reaching information pages.

Computers: World Wide Web: Beginner's Guides

- Internet Beginner's Guides@ *(11)*

- A Beginner's Guide to HTML [*] - from ncsa. A good guide for beginners
- A Primer for creating Web Resources - Good meta-index for html/web creation info
- Bare Bones Guide to HTML [new]
- DWB's WWW Authoring Info - A listing of only the most useful documents to the WWW author, organized into a wide variety of subjects.
- Easy Mosaic and Introductory Web Surfing
- Eine Einführung in das World Wide Web - An Introduction for German Users - Covers the whole WWW features
- Spinning the Web: Setting Up World Wide Web Server
- Starting to use the Web

Figure 8.5 A good place to start your explorations of the Web! Start from Yahoo and select Computers, then World Wide Web, then Beginner's Guides. These items at this level are all active pages, mainly outside the Yahoo site.

If there is no number after the item, selecting that takes you directly to a page. There may be other hypertext links on that page, but they are outside of the Yahoo directory structure. If you had the time and the patience, you could prabably get to everywhere on the Web from a Yahoo start point!

GNN

GNN (Global Network Navigator) is provided by the publishers O'Reilly & Associates. They offer six routes into the Internet:

● **The Whole Internet Catalog** – the main directory.
● **What's New** – a collection of new pages.
● **Best of the Net** – showing what can be done with a little effort and ingenuity.

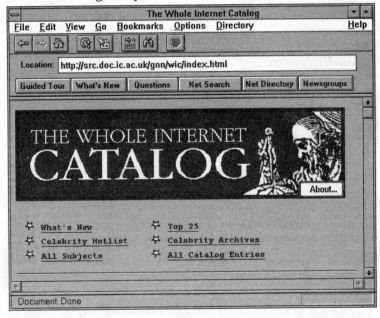

Figure 8.6 GNN's Whole Internet Catalog. The main index is further down this page. GNN's URL is http:/src.doc.ic.ac.uk/gnn/gnn.html.

- **GNN Direct** – on-line shopping, mainly for their books.
- **Business Pages** – linking to many commercial enterprises.
- **Netizens** – a compilation of personal home pages. If you set up a home page, let GNN know about it.

The Whole Internet Catalog is organised by subject under a few major headings, with 15 – 20 sub-headings under each. For example:

→ **Arts & Entertainment**
Architecture - Art Exhibits - Cartoons - Digital Images - E-Zines - Humor - Magazines - Movies - Music - Newspapers - Photography - Radio - Science Fiction - Sound Files - Television - Theater

The other major headings are:

→ **Business & Finance**
→ **Computers**
→ **Education**
→ **Government**
→ **Health & Medicine**
→ **Humanities**
→ **Internet**
→ **Recreation, Sports & Hobbies**
→ **Science & Technology**
→ **Social Sciences**
→ **Travel**

The same style of double-level menu is used at lower levels of the system, and it proves to be an effective way of getting to pages quickly. For instance, it takes only three selections – *Government, Executive Branch, Welcome to the White House* to reach the *Interactive Citizen's Handbook*.

If the home page of your service provider is not a good jumping off point into the World Wide Web, open the *Preferences – Styles* panel and set your Home Page location to either:

GNN http://src.doc.ic.ac.uk/gnn/gnn.html

or

Yahoo   http://www.yahoo.com

Figure 8.7 Welcome to the White House! The current US government uses the Internet actively and attractively. The hyperlinks are embedded in the graphics of this page, and if you have a sound card, you can hear the Welcome Messages.

WEB TO NO 10?

There is no direct link to the UK government through GNN. But if you want to see what it is doing on the Web, you can reach it through Yahoo's International Governments index, or direct to *http://www.open.gov.uk*.

8.5 Using URLs

If you know the Uniform Resource Locator of a page, you can jump directly to it.

Use the *File – Open Location* command, or the 🖳 icon, and type the URL into the slot in the panel.

File	
<u>N</u>ew Window	Ctrl+N
Open <u>L</u>ocation...	**Ctrl+L**
Open <u>F</u>ile...	Ctrl+O
<u>S</u>ave as...	Ctrl+S
<u>M</u>ail Document...	Ctrl+M
<u>C</u>lose	Ctrl+W
E<u>x</u>it	

Note that the address is given without the leading *http:*. That simply identifies it as a World Wide Web URL. Thus the URL:

http://www.yahoo.com

is entered as:

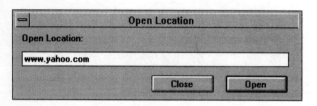

URLs must be typed exactly right for the routine to work. They are not case-sensitive – WWW.YAHOO.COM works just as well as www.yahoo.com – but watch out for symbols. Some URLs include a tilde ~ and some end with slash /.

Finding URLs

Before you can use a URL, you have to know it. There are several possible sources:

- As you browse the Web, you may find a hyperlink to a page that you do not want to visit at the time, but might like to drop in on later. Point to it, to display its URL in the Status bar, and make a note of it.

- If you join any newsgroups (Section 9), you will regularly see postings about relevant pages on the newsgroup area of interest, particularly new ones.
- Internet magazines and newspaper columns often have what's new features.

8.6 Bookmarks

It would be tedious to have to type in the URL of a location every time, if you visited it regularly. Fortunately, you do not have to. Netscape runs a Bookmark system, where the titles and URLs of locations can be stored so that you can then jump to one by picking its title from a list.

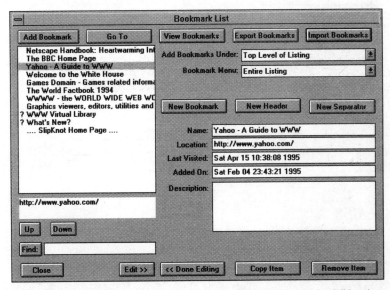

Figure 8.8 The Bookmarks panel is in two parts. Only the left side is visible when you first open it with View Bookmarks. Clicking the Edit button produces the full panel. New bookmarks can be created off-line by typing their names and URLs into the slots on the right.

Adding Bookmarks

There are two ways in which you can add new bookmarks to the current list.

Use the *Add bookmark* command while you are on a Web page, and its title and URL of the current page are added to the list.

Whether you are on- or off-line at the time, you can also add bookmarks by using the *View Bookmarks* command to open the Bookmarks panel. There you can type in the URL and title (make up a suitable one if you do not know it – the title is only to remind you of the page's contents). Clicking New Bookmark will put it into the list.

Bookmark files

It is important to note that bookmarks can be saved as a file – indeed you must save them if you want to retain them from one session to another. They are not saved automatically, as are the Preferences settings. At some point before you exit from Netscape, open the Bookmarks panel and select Export Bookmarks

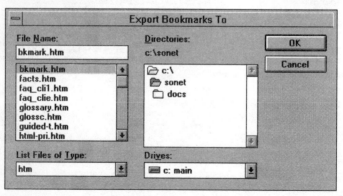

Figure 8.9 Exporting a set of bookmarks to a file. Note the htm (Hypertext Markup Language) extension. This is essential.

When you want to reuse the bookmarks during another session, use `Import Bookmarks` on this panel and select the file.

You can build one single bookmark file, though this is likely to become ungainly after a while. It is probably better to create a separate file for each set of bookmarks that relate to a different aspect of your travels around the Web.

Once bookmarks have been added, or a file imported, they appear as items on the *Bookmark* menu. A couple of clicks is all it takes then to jump to one of your favourite places.

```
Bookmarks
  Add Bookmark                                    Ctrl+A
  View Bookmarks...                               Ctrl+B

  Netscape Handbook: Heartwarming Introduction
  The BBC Home Page
  Yahoo - A Guide to WWW
  Welcome to the White House
  Games Domain - Games related information site
  The World Factbook 1994
  WWWW - the WORLD WIDE WEB WORM
  Graphics viewers, editors, utilities and info
  WWW Virtual Library
  What's New?
  .... SlipKnot Home Page ....
```

Figure 8.10 Imported Bookmarks are added to the drop down menu. Here are the URLs for some of those on my list – others are given elsewhere in this book:

Netscape Handbook	http://home.mcom.com/home/manual_docs/intro.html
The BBC Home Page	http://www.bbcnc.org.uk/
The CIA World Factbook	http://www.ic.gov/94fact/fb94toc/fb94toc.html
Graphic utilities	http://www2.ncsu.edu/bae/people/faculty/walker/ hotlist/graphics.html
WWW Virtual Library	info.cern.ch/hypertext/DataSources/bySubject/ Overview.html

If you are an organised person and have a lot of bookmarks, you can arrange them into a multi-level menu by adding headers and separators – but I'll leave that to you.

——— 8.7 Helper Applications———

Netscape can display most of the graphics and formatted text that it meets on the Web, but there are some for which it needs help – hence the Helper Applications. These are programs that Netscape can call upon to deal with specified types of files. For example, if you want to view video clips that you find on the Web, and have QuickTime, MpegPlay or another suitable video player, this can be linked into Netscape as a viewer. (If you do not have one, you can track down a player program with **Archie** (10.2) and download it with **ftp** (11.2).

Figure 8.11 The Helper Applications panel, at the start of adding a new viewer to handle postscript files.

Follow these steps to add a viewer:

1 Use the *Options – Preference* command and switch to the Helper Applications panel.
2 Scan through the file types and extensions in the *Mime type* list to find one for which you have a suitable viewer.
3 Select it, to copy the *Extensions* into the slot.
4 Click on Browse and hunt through your directories for the program.
5 Set the Launch option if you want the program to be called up when Netscape meets one of these files, or Save if you would prefer to store it on disk for later viewing.
6 Go back to step 2 for the next file type or exit with OK.

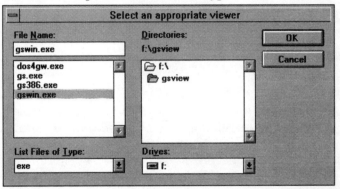

Figure 8.12 Browsing for a viewer – here Ghostview, a postscript viewer is being selected.

WHICH VIEWERS?

Don't try to find a viewer for every file! There are some types that you will never need, others that you will meet only rarely. Start with those that you can deal with easily – perhaps the avi (Audio-Visual) and wav (Soundwave) files that can be handled by the Windows MultiMedia Player, MPLAYER.EXE. (Note that you will need Soundblaster or its equivalent for the sound files.)

8.8 Searching the Web

You can find most things by browsing through one or other of the net directories, but it can sometimes take a while – especially if you are researching an esoteric topic, or if you want to track down all the pages that relate to a topic. This is where the search engines and Web crawlers come into play. They are designed to hunt systematically through the Web to track down pages that meet your specifications.

There are a number of tools that search in different ways and through different aspects of the Internet. Some are easier to access and to use than others.

Net Search

If you use Netscape, start by clicking | Net Search |. This connects you to the InfoSeek page at Netscape's home site which has brief but useful descriptions and links to several search engines. Among these, you will find *InfoSeek Search*. Point and click into the slot to locate the cursor, then type a word or two to describe what you are looking for. Try to be as specific as possible, and to avoid words that could be embedded in others.

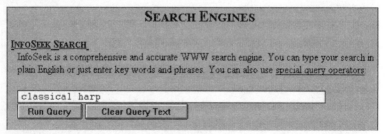

Figure 8.13 Part of the InfoSeek home page at the start of making a query. If you do not have Netscape and want to use InfoSeek, you can reach it at the URL: http://www.infoseek.com.

On this search, for example, looking for articles on classical harp music, 'classical' and 'harp' should focus the search well, though in fact it also brought up 'Harper', a company that makes necks for guitars! The Harper page presumably contained a reference to 'classical' guitars.

Click **Run Query** to start the search. There will be a delay of a few moments while the system connects to the InfoSeek server and runs the program, before the Search Results page appears.

The page shows 10 'hits' from the query, giving for each the title of the Web page along with the first few lines of text – these are very useful as the title alone is sometimes not enough to tell you much about a page. The other, and very essential piece of information that is shown is the URL of each page.

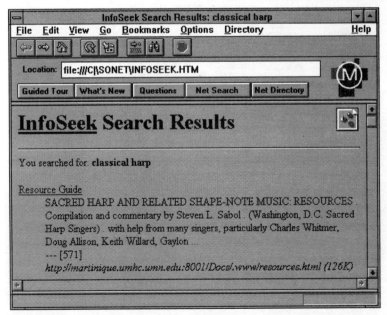

Figure 8.14 The InfoSeek Search Results page shows the titles, first few lines and the URLs of 10 pages that match your search criteria.

The Web Crawler

Another possible start point is at the University of Geneva, where they have a collection of search tools under the heading *W3 Search Engines*. The URL is:

http://cuiwww.unige.ch/meta-index.html

If you work your way down the page a little, you will meet a section headed *Spider-based WWW Catalogs*.

The first of the tools here is the Web Crawler. This is used in much the same way as InfoSeek. Type a word or words into the slot, to define your search. In the example I am again looking for any pages on *classical harp* music. The *AND words together box* is checked so that the search is for those pages on which

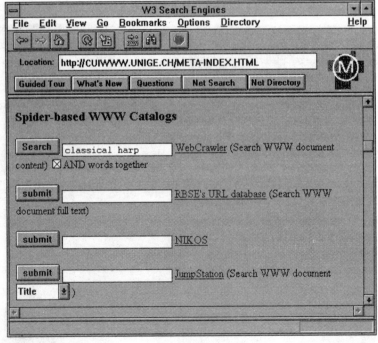

Figure 8.15 Starting a search with the Web Crawler.

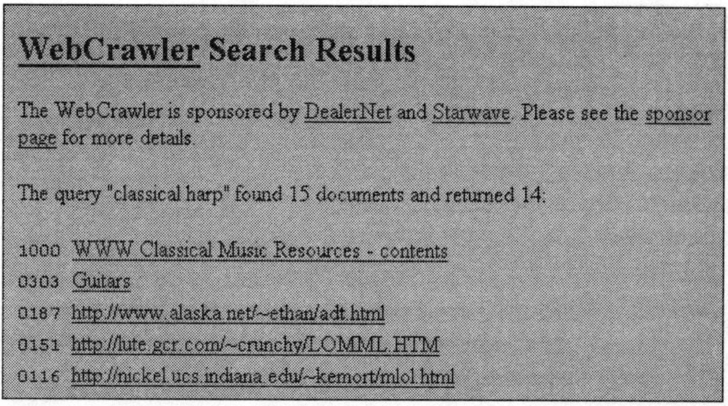

WebCrawler Search Results

The WebCrawler is sponsored by DealerNet and Starwave. Please see the sponsor page for more details.

The query "classical harp" found 15 documents and returned 14:

1000 WWW Classical Music Resources - contents
0303 Guitars
0187 http://www.alaska.net/~ethan/adt.html
0151 http://lute.gcr.com/~crunchy/LOMML.HTM
0116 http://nickel.ucs.indiana.edu/~kemort/mlol.html

Figure 8.16 Getting results from the Web Crawler. This gives the URLs of relevant pages, but no other details. If you want to go straight to the Web Crawler, its URL is http://webcrawler.cs.washington.edu/cgi-bin/WebQuery.html.

the words 'classical' AND 'harp' are found. If the AND box was not checked, the search would be for pages containing either 'classical' OR 'harp' – which would have produced more than I wanted, much of it off-topic.

Clicking **Search** sends the query off to the Web Crawler, and after a few moments you should get a results page listing the URLs of those pages that match your search criteria. If there are no matches, try again with less stringent criteria.

The Web Crawler's results page is not as informative as that of InfoSeek. You only get the URLs of related pages, but at least it does not restrict you to 10 hits.

─────── 8.9 The Internet Mall ───────

I have used the word 'Mall' in the heading to emphasise the predominance of the US in this as in most other areas of the Internet. If you go to *Yahoo* (http://www.yahoo.com) and browse

Apparel/Accessories	Gourmet Foods
Audio Equipment	Gifts
Automotive	Health Products
Books	Hobbies & Entertainment
Business Services	Household Goods
Cameras/Optical Equipment	Jewelry
Children's Clothes & Goods	Magazines & Periodicals
Collectibles	Office Equipment
Computer Hardware	Tapes & Compact Discs
Computer Peripherals	Sporting Equipment
Computer Software	Telecommunications
Computer Services	Travel
Financial	Video Cassettes & Discs
Flowers & Plants	Video Equipment

Table 8.1 This listing from CompuServe's shopping directory should give an idea of the range of products and services that can be purchased on-line.

through their *Business / Electronic Commerce / Shopping Centers* pages, you will find companies offering products and services that stretch from children's toys and clothes through to funerals. The coverage is not quite 'from the cradle to the grave', for there are large gaps in between. The on-line stores do not always live up to the promise of their names – for example, the *Global Shopping Network* (http://www.gsn.com), specialises in equipment for sailors and deep sea anglers; *Sell-it on the WWW* (http://www.xmission.com/~wwwads) is one of many small organisations that deal largely in arts and craft gifts. It seems ironic that high-tech is used to sell low-tech!

The main problem about selling over the World Wide Web is that you cannot feel, try on or try out most products over a modem link. You cannot even see goods conveniently, given the time it takes to download graphics and the relatively low resolution of images. There are marketing opportunities on the Web, but the things which are sold tend to be those products and services which might otherwise be sold by mail order or telephone, or those which arise directly out of the Internet. Web pages are seen as effective adverts for companies in Internet

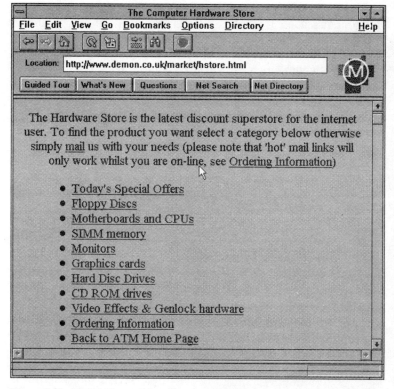

Figure 8.17 What better way to sell computers than by computer! This is the top page of ATM, at http://www.demon.co.uk/market.

services, computer hardware and software, book, record and video publishing, IT training, consultancy and the like – your presence on the Web is proof that yours is a modern business.

A second problem has been the security of on-line credit-card transactions. A few well-publicised cases of credit-card fraud and of hackers accessing list of card numbers have made people cautious about on-line transactions. Recent improvements in security appear to have made this as safe as telephone or mail-order transactions, but confidence will take time to build.

On-line shopping has not yet really taken off in the UK. At present there are a few UK-based companies offering a limited range of consumer goods and services over the Web. You can, for example, buy computer hardware and software from *ATM* (http://www.demon.co.uk/market); computer books and manuals from US and UK publishers from *Computer Manuals Ltd* (www.demon.co.uk/compman) or house insurance, legal services, books, travel bookings, flowers, cakes, teddy bears and other gifts from *MarketNet Services* (http://mkn.co.uk/).

───── 8.10 On-line Games ─────

If you want to see what kind of games are available on-line, take a trip to *Yahoo* and select *Entertainment*, then *Games*. The first part of this page (below) shows just 9 of the 80+ entries, but these include some typical examples.

All New Castle Gormenghast is one of a number of compendiums of simple computer games – elsewhere you will find several implementations of Hangman, Battleships and the like. If you need to fill in time (while you are paying for it on the phone), then you can.

Air Warrior is an interactive flight simulator, with the added bonus of your being able to 'fly' alongside others – and to shoot them down! To play, you have to download the game, to run on your machine, and sign up with one of the hosts that handles the interactions. In the UK, the main service is Delphi. They offer a few hours free trial to prospective members, but watch out – if you get addicted, Air Warrior costs around 50p an hour to play, on top of the normal charges. Delphi can be contacted at 0171 757 7080 or e-mail at *ukservice@delphi.com*.

The *Backgammon* and *Billiards* entries are mainly on-line clubs for where enthusiasts can discuss strategies, organise conventions and generally keep in touch with one another. Chess, Go,

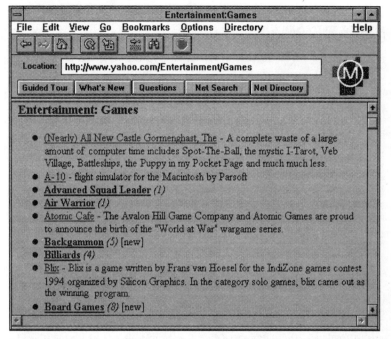

Figure 8.18 Part of the top level Games page at Yahoo. Over 600 entries can be accessed from here.

Othello, Scrabble and other popular games all have similar 'clubs'. Some of these run e-mail or real-time games between members.

Board Games are good sources of shareware and commercial software implementations of board games.

The other main type of games, not visible on this part of the Games page, are interactive adventures. There are, for instance, over 150 MUDs (Multi-User Dungeon) and MUSHes (Multi-User Shared Hallucinations) on the Web. Some of these are purely text games, others have graphics (if you can wait for them); some are played within a tightly structured world, some are designed to be changed by the users as they play.

If you want to try out a MUD, you can play free of charge by logging in to Aladdin:

Tel:01703 393700
Communications: 8 Data bits, No parity, 1 Stop bit.
Login as *mudguest1*.

GAMES DOMAIN

In the UK, the best collection of games is probably the one at Birmingham University, but be prepared for difficulty in logging in as it is popular! Add this URL to your Bookmarks:

http://wcl-rs.bham.ac.uk/GamesDomain.

8.11 Spry Mosaic

Spry Mosaic is the Web browser supplied by CompuServe to its members. In all practical respects it is the same as Netscape, though there are superficial differences and some additions that generally make it even easier to use. It is not as good as Netscape in one respect. In Netscape you can click a hyperlink and start to load the linked page while the current page is still being loaded. Spry Mosaic makes you wait until it has finished loading a page before allowing you to open the next.

If you compare Spry Mosaic's screen with that of **Netscape** (8.3), you will see that there are equivalent buttons on each, but with three new ones here.

 switches into *kiosk* mode, where the whole screen is used for displaying the Web page. This can be useful sometimes. The normal screen with its commands and icons can be restored by pressing <Escape>.

The other two icons are related to **Hotlinks** (below).

Figure 8.19 CompuServe's home page has hyperlinks embedded in the graphic –
if you prefer to keep the automatic loading of images off, the same links are present
in the text.

Configuring Spry Mosaic

This is amazingly easy – in fact, you do not have to do anything
is you already have WinCIM installed. The setup routine will
extract all the relevant details about you and your connection
from the WinCIM files. The only thing you might like to do is to
check the *Viewer* list, on the *Options* menu, and add any additional viewers that you may have. There is a much shorter list
of viewer types here than in Netscape, but they include all the
commonly found types – more can be added if needed.

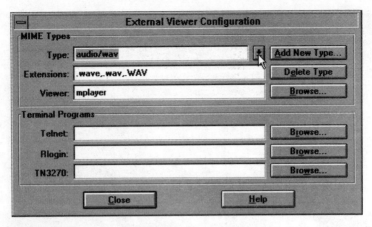

Figure 8.20 To configure an additional viewer for Spry Mosaic you would normally just select the Type, then Browse for the program.

Hotlinks and Hotlists

Hotlinks are the equivalent of Bookmarks, and Hotlists the equivalent of Bookmark files. They are implemented in a way that makes them easier for the novice, though more experienced users may prefer the greater flexibility of the Netscape system.

 The Hotlist button, and the *File – Hotlists* command, open a panel, where you can edit or configure your hotlists. You do not need to load the hotlist files – that is done automatically, as is saving them if you have added new items. That is a great advantage to those of us who tend to end the session then remember that we forgot to save our new Bookmarks.

Spry Mosaic comes with a dozen or so ready-made hotlists, each containing hotlinks to a set of related pages. Amongst others there are *Business, Internet Information, Shopping, Travel* and *Computer Geek* (if anyone will admit to being one!). All together there must be around 100 hotlinks, which provide a wide and varied range of jumping off points for your travels.

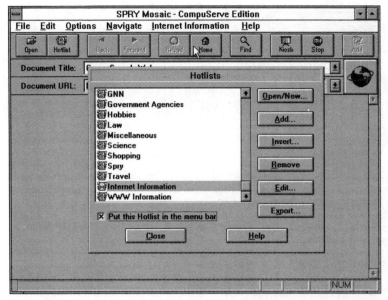

Figure 8.21 The Hotlists panel in Spry Mosaic, displaying part of the ready made set of hotlists. Notice that *Internet Information* has been added to the menu bar. When it is no longer needed, selecting it and clearing the checkbox will remove it from the bar.

If these are not enough for you, the **Open/New...** button can be used to set up a new hotlist, and new links can be added to a chosen hotlist by clicking **Add...** and typing the page title and URL into a little dialog box. The alternative – and simpler – simpler way to add a new page is to click the Add button on the main screen when you are on that page.

The Hotlists panel offers the option of putting a hotlist on to the menu bar, making that set of hotlinks instantly accessible. To do this you simply select the hotlist from the display and click the option box. A second click will remove the checkmark and take the hotlist off the menu.

———— 8.12 Summary ————

- The Web consists of pages linked together by URLs embedded in the hypertext of the pages.

- Many pages contain graphics. Turning off the automatic downloading of images will significantly speed up your work.

- Netscape is a powerful, but remarkably easy to use Web browser.

- Several organisations run Net Directories to help you find your way around; Yahoo and GNN are among the most comprehensive of these.

- If you know the URL of a page, Open Location will take you straight to it.

- If you find a page you want to revisit, you can add it to a Bookmark list – it will then be just a couple of clicks away.

- You must remember to export your Bookmarks to disk if you want to reuse them another time.

- If needed, more viewers can be linked in as Helper Applications.

- The Web Crawler, InfoSeek and other search engines can be used to track down pages containing key words.

- Some goods and services can be purchased on-line, but the range is limited as yet.

- There are many on-line individual and interactive games that you can play – some purely time-wasting, others challenging, even addictive!

- CompuServe offers the Spry Mosaic Web browser to its members. It is very similar to Netscape, but geared to make it even easier for the novice.

9

NEWSGROUPS

— 9.1 Aims of this chapter —

Newsgroups, mailing lists and forums are the clubs of the Internet. They are where people come together to share common interests and enthusiasms, to ask for and to give help, to debate and to announce new discoveries and creations. There are thousands of them, each devoted to a different topic, ranging from the seriously academic to the totally trivial.

As a subscriber to a newsgroup you can:

● read articles by other people
● post your own articles
● respond to articles, either by e-mailing a reply directly to the author, or by posting a follow-up article to the group.

In this chapter we will dip into this vast pool of newsgroups, see how to join a group and how to behave as a member – knowing your netiquette is important. We will also see it in practice through three different systems. **WinNET News** (9.6) is typical of the off-line approach; **Netscape** (9.7) lets you access the news through the Web; **Compuserve** (9.8) also brings you the Internet's news and has its own forums for communication.

— 9.2 Newsgroups and Mailing lists —

Newsgroups and mailing lists are two approaches to the same end – that of distributing a message from one person to all the others in the 'club'. The differences between them are largely in the ways that they are organised. With a mailing list an individual copy of each message is sent to each subscriber; with newsgroups, the articles are transferred in bulk between the sites that act as news servers, and are distributed from there to the subscribers. The main differences that you will notice as a user is that you subscribe to them in slightly different ways, and you handle maillists through your normal e-mail system, while newsgroups need news reader software.

If you join CompuServe, you will have access to their **forums** (9.8) as well as to the Internet's maillist and newsgroups. Similar systems for sharing ideas and news are offered by many of the other larger on-line service providers.

Usenet Newsgroups

Most newsgroups are part of the Usenet system, one of the networks that merged to form the Internet and one that had used newsgroups as its major communications tool. Some have come in from other networks, notably ClariNet and Fido (based in Germany); others have been started set up more recently.

There are over 6,000 Usenet and other newsgroups that can be accessed over the Internet. They are organised into about 20 major divisions, subdivided by topic, and subdivided again where necessary.

Their names reflect this structure and describe their focus; thus, for example, *rec.art.animation* is found in the *art* sub-division of the *rec* main division and is devoted to animation as an art form. (There are other animation groups elsewhere, with different focuses.)

Note that the dots in a name do not always reflect the hierarchical structure. They are sometimes used for punctuation, and sometimes just for fun. Next to *alt.wired* (for the enthusiastic) you will find *alt.wired.tired.tired.tired* (for the exhausted).

With so many groups, it is not possible to cover them all here – that would take a whole book (and months of research!) – but the following brief survey should give some indication of the scope of newsgroups, and where to start looking for ones that might interest you.

alt – the alternative newsgroups, set up to cover topics that had not been included in the other main divisions. This set is enormous both in number and in range, so if you can't find a newsgroup anywhere else, try alt. Hobbies, obsessions and fan clubs form a substantial part of the alt groups, though there are also groups for specialist software, professional interests and discussions. Dipping into those starting with a.. we find:

alt.aldus.freehand

Discussions, tips, problems and solutions for users of the Aldus design/drawing package.

alt.alien.visitors

For people who have met them or are looking for them and are struggling against the government conspiracy to suppress the facts. Join it and find out the truth – but watch your phone bills mount as a huge volume of articles pour in every day!

alt.animation.warner-bros

Another animation group, for a different set of fans.

alt.architecture.int-design
alt.aromatherapy

These two are adjacent in the listings, but neatly show the diversity of interests.

biz – business-oriented groups. Here you will find announcements of new products, offers of services, job opportunities and discussions of market-related issues.

comp – a large set of newsgroups which gives a good example of the subdivided structure. It covers many aspects of computing, including languages, applications, hardware and standards among its 70 first level divisions. One of these *comp.sys* then splits 42 ways, each devoted to a different hardware system.

If we focus on the *comp.sys.ibm* groups, we find two subsets – one for PCs and one for PS2s. *comp.sys.ibm.pc* then divides

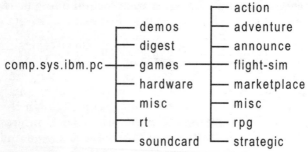

comp.sys.ibm.pc
- demos
- digest
- games
  - action
  - adventure
  - announce
  - flight-sim
  - marketplace
  - misc
  - rpg
  - strategic
- hardware
- misc
- rt
- soundcard

info – a fairly small but very mixed set of newsgroups, with discussions ranging from the politics of firearms control to the management of Sun computer systems, but with a core focusing on NSF, the National Science Foundation network whose hardware forms the backbone of the Internet in the US.

mail – largely devoted to technical aspects of e-mail systems.

misc – miscellaneous. Books, health, education, kids, for sale and job opportunities (all US-based) make up the bulk of these.

news – amongst these newsgroups about newsgroups you will find several specaially for new users. *news.announce.newusers* and *news.newusers* are good sources of tips and advice, while *news.answers* may solve your problems. If you can't find an answer there, ask in *news.newusers.questions*.

rec – a very large set covering the whole range of recreational activities from arts through games to sports, with virtually everything in between. These three give an idea of the diversity:

rec.arts.sf.tv.quantum-leap
rec.games.xtank.programmer
rec.gardens.orchids

sci – academic and professional scientific discussion groups.

soc – most of the groups here are for discussions of different cultures, religions and social issues.

talk – mainly about politics, with some religion and philosophy.

Non-Usenet newsgroups include sets run through *bionet* (biological sciences), *clarinet* (mainly US business and regional news), *eunet* (European), *gnu* (Unix systems), and *ieee* (international standards body for electronics). There are also sets of groups for Australia, Brazil, Canada, Germany, France and the UK. Join *uk.events* to find out what's going on, or *uk.jobs.offered* if you are looking for opportunities in the computing industry.

Moderation

Most newsgroups are *moderated* – they have someone to check incoming articles and weed out the irrelevant ones before distribution. Others are *unmoderated*, and with these the only restriction is that you must be a subscriber to be able to submit articles. Moderation is not really necessary for those groups on a specialised academic or professional topic, as the quantity of articles tends to be low – and the quality high. With popular newsgroups – those that are devoted to TV shows, pop stars, sports and more or less anything to do with sex – moderation is essential. Even with the irrelevant filtered out, the quantity of articles generated in some of these groups has to be downloaded to be believed – and the quality is highly variable.

Mailing lists

When you join a mailing list, you get the messages sent directly to you from the list's moderator – not personally, it is all automated! To subscribe, you must mail a request to the list server on the moderator's machine – you should be able to get a list of these from your service provider. Address the message to listserv@name_of_server and carry the line:

```
SUBSCRIBE   your_name   your_e-mail_address
```

——— 9.3 Being a News Reader ———

An article has four components:

> the title or *subject line*;
> the *e-mail address* of its author;
> the *body text*, which may be anything from a single line to
> many pages;
> the *signature* of its author.

A newsgroup may generate anything from two or three to a
hundred articles every day. Even if you are fascinated by the
topic of the newsgroup, you are unlikely to want to read every
article, and that is where the subject line comes in. Your news
reader software will display the subject and author of the articles in a list. Scanning through the subject lines should give
you a clear idea of the nature of the articles, and whether or
not you want to read them.

Having **read** an article, you may be stimulated to respond. You
can do this in two ways – either sending e-mail to the author
only, or posting a follow-up article to the group. In general, if
the original article was a request for information – where can I
find *whatnot* software? – you should reply to the author only,
as this is not likely to be of general interest.

If you want to **follow up** on an article with your own contribu-
tion to the discussion, you would normally quote the relevant
lines from the original article or give a brief summary of the
key points that you want to pick up.

If you want to put out your own request for information, or to
start a new discussion, then you **post** your article to the group.

Don't rush into posting articles. There are few things existing
members find more irritating than a newbie asking obvious
questions or rehearsing old arguments. Take time to read
enough to pick up the true flavour of the group and to find out
what topics have been discussed recently. Take time also to
track down the group's Frequently Asked Questions list – this

is posted regularly in most groups. Most groups also maintain a collection or a digest of old articles. Find the most recent ones and scan them to see what has been covered before you post.

Reading without posting is known as **lurking**. It's OK to lurk. Some groups, especially the smaller and more intense discussion groups dislike lurkers – they see it almost as a form of eavesdropping – but even here it is better to lurk until you have got into the swing of things..

The **signature** is optional. Not everybody uses one, and among those that do, some keep them very simple – real name or nickname and e-mail address; people who have Internet access through an organisation often use it to include a disclaimer that the views expressed are personal, and not those of the organisation; others include snappy quotations or ASCII art – pictures composed of letters and symbols.

Figure 9.1 A good example of ASCII art in a signature – slightly on the long side, but the quality makes it worth it.

DECODING BINARIES

If you join any *binaries* newsgroups, you will get articles with embedded binary files – mainly graphics and sounds. To extract these, follow the same procedures as for **Binary files by mail** (7.9). Sometimes the files will be too large to fit in one article. With these, you must first cut out the encoded blocks and reassemble them in a word-processor, before attempting to decode them.

——— 9.4 Newsgroup Netiquette ———

Like much of the rest of the Internet the Newsgroup system relies on cooperation, voluntary labour, some sponsorship and a set of agreed rules – its *netiquette*. Take the trouble to learn the rules and use them. Using netiquette is not just about being a good news user – it is also a matter of self-preservation. The thing to remember is that, with a popular group, any article you write is going to be downloaded by several thousand people, and many of these will be paying phone and on-line charges for receiving your article. If you waste their time and money, they will not be happy and may well respond with *flames* – angry mail. Follow the rules and make life easier for others and for yourself.

1 **Do** KISS – Keep It Short and Simple. Keep it short to save bandwidth and phone time; keep it simple because the Internet is an international community and not all users speak English as their first language – and even those that do are of mixed ability and ages.

2 **Do** top and tail thoughtfully. Write a clear and descriptive subject line, and don't overdo your signature.

3 **Do** be relevant. Every newsgroup has its own focus; if what you want to say is not within its focus, find one where it does fit. Straying off-topic will get you flamed.

4 **Do** watch the humour. Irony and subtle jokes don't always travel well in brief, written messages. If there is any possibility of a humorous comment being misunderstood, add a **smiley** (9.5).

5 **Do** read any follow-ups to an article – the subject line will have **Re:** before the original title – before writing yours. Someone else may already have made the same points.

6 **Do** summarise, or crop the copy of the original article when following up.

7 **Don't** overreact to others. Ignore bad spelling and poor grammar – this is a mixed, multi-lingual community (see 1 above); if you spot crass mistakes, drop the writers a quiet

e-mail, don't humiliate them in public; if you are angered by a particularly offensive or bigoted article, wait until you are calm, and write a reasoned rebuttal.

8 **Don't** use the newsgroups to advertise, except in those that are for advertising – the 'for sales', business announcements and the like.

9 **Don't** send an article more than once. There is little point in repeating one across a set of related newsgroups as many of them cross-post to each other automatically.

10 **Don't** post reviews of books or films that reveal the plot, or jokes that might offend tender sensibilities, without first encoding the article with *rot13*.

---

rot13

This is a simple letter-substitution code designed to give users the choice of whether or not to read a message. To decode the text, exchange each letter with the one at the equivalent place in the other half of the alphabet – A to M move 13 places on, N to Z, 13 places back. Decoding programs are very easy to write, or use this to decode by hand:

A B C D E F G H I J K L M N O P Q R S T U V W X Y Z
Z Y X W V U T S R Q P O N M L K J I H G F E D C B A

— 9.5 Smileys and other conventions —

Being good news users (and perhaps indifferent typists?), we try to keep our articles short – abbreviations help here. But as we keep them short, and as we may not know our potential readers very well, if at all, there is a chance of our attempts at humour being misunderstood. Smileys were developed to help to overcome this.

Smileys

Smileys – also called *emoticons* – are the equivalent of the facial expressions that we use to the emotions or hidden meanings behind what we say. They are little pictures, composed of ASCII characters, intended to convey these expressions.

The basic smiley of :–) is the one you will see most often, though there are many other weird and wonderful smileys around.

:-)	The basic smiley, saying "Don't take this seriously"
'-)	Wink – "Only joking!"
:-(	Frowning or sad
:-o	Wow!
:-|	Grim
:-C	"I don't believe it!"
(-:	User is left handed
%-)	User has been staring at a screen for hours
8-)	User is wearing sunglasses

Figure 9.2 A collection of smileys. The top set are in common use. The ones below are examples of some of the many others that you may meet.

Abbreviations

These are mainly used in real-time conferences and chat lines, though some crop up quite regularly in newsgroup articles.

BBS	Bulletin Board System
BTW	By The Way
BWQ	Buzz Word Quotient
DL	DownLoad
FYI	For Your Information
GIGO	Garbage In Garbage Out
IMO	In My Opinion

IMHO   In My Humble Opinion (typically used ironically)
MOTOS   Member Of The Opposite Sex
MOTSS   Member Of The Same Sex
POV   Point Of View
RPG   Role Playing Games
RTFM   Read The F***ing Manual
TIA   Thanks In Advance
TTFN   Ta Ta For Now
UL   UpLoad
WRT   With Reference To
<g>   Grin

If you want to track down more abbreviations or the acronyms used elsewhere in the computing world, an excellent list called Babel is maintained by Irving Kind at Temple University in the States. Get a copy by **ftp** (11.2) at this URL:

ftp.temple.edu/pub/info/help-net/babel95a.txt

Emphasis

The other problem that we have in writing articles or e-mail is that only plain ASCII text can be transmitted. You cannot underline or embolden words. If you want to make a word stand out, enclose it in *asterisks* or _underlines_, or use CAPITALS.

9.6 WinNET News

If all you really want from the Internet is access to e-mail and the newsgroups, then joining WinNet is the cheapest and the best option. Their WinNet Tools software has simple-to-use but very effective facilities for handling newsgroups.

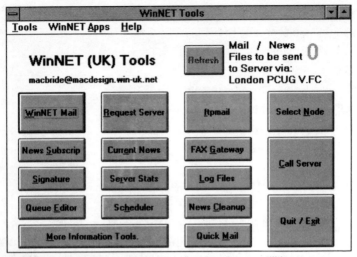

Figure 9.3 WinNet Tools is a collection of mail and news utilities.

Subscribing

Run WinNet Tools and click ⌷News Subscrip⌷ to start the subscription utility. The left hand pane of its window shows you the newsgroup to which you currently subscribe; the right hand pane is where list of newsgroups is displayed when you are searching for a new one.

When you are trying to subscribe to a new group, the first job is to find it. At the top of this pane is a slot for the search criteria – this will be part of a name. The drop-down list at this slot carries a set of part-names, but if you are hunting for something special, such as all groups that have *animation* in their names, this could be typed in.

Clicking ⌷Search⌷ starts a searching through the list of active groups. Any that contain a match will be listed in the display area. If you select one and click ⌷Subscribe⌷, the utility generates a subscription request and mails it to the newsgroup server

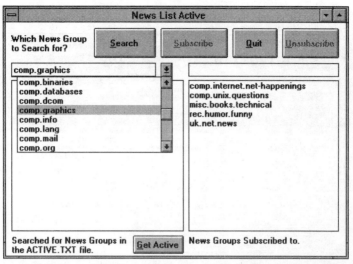

Figure 9.4 Picking criteria from the drop-down list before starting a search for a newsgroup. In this example, we are looking for those in the comp.graphics set.

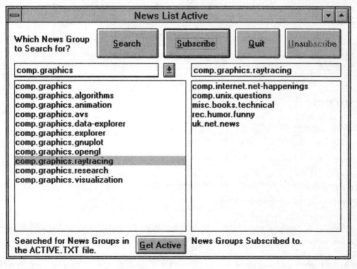

Figure 9.5 WinNet Tools pick-and-click approach makes such easy work of subscribing to a new group.

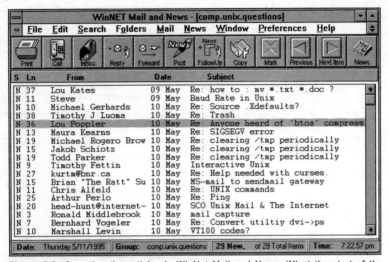

Figure 9.6 Scanning the articles in WinNet Mail and News. 'N' at the start of the line indicates a new (unread) article.

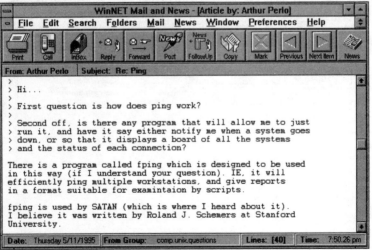

Figure 9.7 Reading an article in WinNet's editor. The one shown here is a follow-up from a previous article. We can tell this by the Re: in the subject line and the lines are marked by > at the start. These have been copied in from the original article. (You may also see : colons and } braces used to indicate copied lines.)

facilities at WinNet next time you dial in. If you want to see exactly what a subscription request looks like, you can view your outgoing mail in the Queue Editor.

News articles should start coming in within a day or so – some are slower as not all the groups have a posting every day. When you use the Call Server to get your mail, it also picks up any news articles. They can then be read, along with your mail in the WinNet Mail software. To get to them, use the **News – News Group List** command and select a group. You will then see a list of articles with their authors, dates and subjects.

Clicking anywhere on an article's line opens the viewer/editor for reading. You have several ways to respond to an article:

- **Reply** sends mail to the author only.
- **Follow-up** sends a response to the group.
- **Post** submits a completely new article.
- **Forward** sends a copy on to someone else.

Reply and Follow-up both offer to copy the original article into your message. If you do accept the offer, trim it down to the bare essentials before adding your own comments.

Cleaning up

News articles build up on your hard disk, just like newspapers build up in the corner of the room. Half a dozen moderately busy newsgroups will generate 100k or more of articles a day. You may want to keep a few of these for future reference, and the Copy button allows you to do this by copying them into another folder, but most you will only want to read once. Every now and then you should run **News Cleanup** to make space.

You can either do a simple **Cleanup**, which removes articles from the folders and from your disk; or an **Archive**, which removes articles from the news folder and packs them into one long – uncompressed – file. If there are a lot of files, the cleanup could take a few minutes.

——— 9.7 Netscape news ———

You can read news articles directly off the Web through Netscape. This approach is good for finding out what newsgroups are around, for getting an idea of the quality, volume and content of the articles in a group, and for researching topics, but is not as efficient as an off-line reader for a regular subscription.

As you travel over the Web, you will often come across a link in a page to a related newsgroup, but if you really want to see what is around, you need to get hold of the full list. Next time you are running Netscape, click the ⟨Newsgroups⟩ button. This takes you to the page where you can link to the newsgroups to which you are subscribed, and to all others. You will probably find that you are already a member of the groups run by your service provider. (Check these regularly for news of the service.)

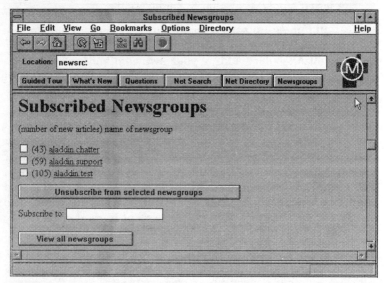

Figure 9.8 Setting up newsgroups in Netscape. At this stage, the only three listed are those run by the service provider, Aladdin. To subscribe to a group, all you have to do is type its name – accurately – in the slot at the bottom.

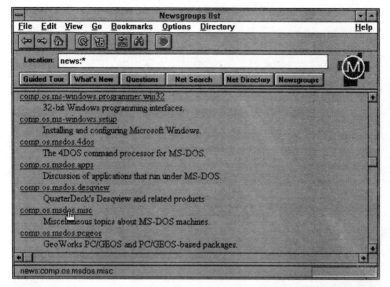

Figure 9.9 Once you have the newsgroup list downloaded, you can dip into them to see what they have to offer.

Click on the ▭ **View all newsgroups** ▭ button to access all the groups supported by your service. This will vary. You will recall that the difference between **newsgroups and mailing lists** (9.2) is that news articles are transferred in bulk between those computers that act as servers, and distributed to subscribers from there. Not all providers accept and distribute all newsgroups – some are specific to individual providers, others are of limited interest and will only only be handled if a user requests subscription.

Be prepared for a wait. The group list is enormous – around 200k – and will take a while to download. When you have got it, save it to file for future reference.

To read the articles in any group, simply click on its name. *Be prepared for another wait*. It takes the system a while to locate the group, download the articles and sort them into order.

What you see next is not a set of individual title lines, as in newsreader software such as WinNet, but a list of 'lead' articles. When you use a newsreader you download the articles that have been posted since you last logged on – and with a busy group this may be as many as a hundred; when you access newsgroups through Netscape, you get the articles that have built up over the previous month – which could run into thousands! Some organisation is essential if readers are to find their way through. The solution is to arrange them into threads – those articles that have been posted as follow-ups to the same one.

Clicking on a lead article's name call it up and takes you into a reading screen. The button controls here let you move between other articles, post a follow-up or mail a reply.

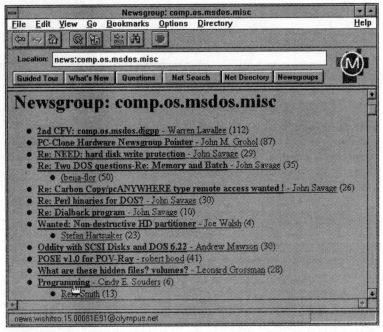

Figure 9.10 Picking up the threads in Netscape news. The number after each title shows how many articles followed on from the original one.

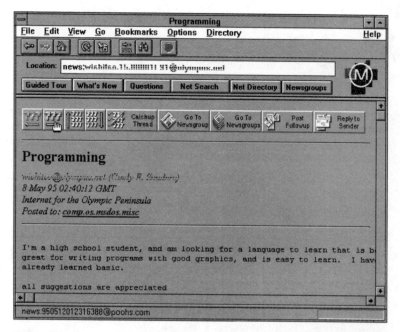

Figure 9.11 News reading in Netscape. The leftmost two buttons move between articles in the thread; the next pair take you to the previous and next lead article. Note the difference between the **Go to newsgroup** button, which takes you to the list of threads, and the **Go to newsgroups** button, which takes you back two stages to the main group listing.

Subscribing

If you find a newsgroup that interests you, and you would like to subscribe to it, make a *careful* note of its name. If you want to continue to read it through Netscape, return to the Subscribed Newsgroups page and type the name into the **Subscribe to:** slot. After you press [Enter] the newsgroup will be added to your list.

If you prefer to use an off-line newsreader for your regular news, then keep that note of the name until you next use your newsreader.

9.8 Compuserve Forums

CompuServe was aiming to provide a comprehensive service before the Internet got going, so it is no surprise to find that they have their own equivalent of newsgroups. The approach was different. They took the view that people with a common interest might want to share files and real-time chat, as well as messages, and that these sharing activities should be grouped under the interest heading. The result was the forums system.

Forums are grouped by topic, with each devoted to one aspect. To get to the PC Fun forum, for example, the simplest route starts with the Fun & Games icon  on the main screen. Selecting Games Forums from its menu opens a second level menu, where the options are all different aspects of games. Selecting PC Fun takes you into the forum. (You will be asked to join the first time you visit.) When you enter it, you have access to a common message board, a library of files and a conference area where members can 'talk' to each other on-line.

Messages

The *Browse* option on the *Messages* menu opens a list of main groupings. The numbers to the right of each line show how many different topics are being discussed and the total number of messages under each heading. Selecting a title takes you to the next level, to pick a topic; the next step takes you to the

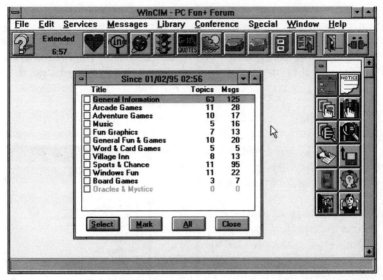

Figure 9.12 Selecting a topic in the message area – the equivalent of picking up a thread in a newsgroup. The icon set on the right gives quick access to the facilties available in the forum system.

first message in the thread, viewed through the same reader that is used in **CompuServe mail** (7.7).

Conferences

There are various 'chat' areas, allowing on-line communication, available on the Internet, but CompuServe's conferences have the special feature that you know you share an interest with the other people that you will meet, as they are members of the same forum.

Don't think that this guarantees you sparkling conversation with fellow enthusiasts. The number of people who are in a forum at any one time can vary enormously, and they are more likely to be reading messages or downloading files than to be looking for a chat. It can work, however, and it can be good.

Libraries

These can be an excellent source of files. The quality varies, reflecting the variety of forum users, but there is plenty of freeware and shareware, as well as updates and bug-fixes from mainstream software companies, and commercial products. In the libraries you will find programs ranging from serious applications and utilities through to games, plus text files, clip art, photographs, and computer graphics, music, video clips and other multimedia resources.

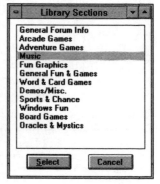

COMPU$ERVE

When you are using CompuServe's forums, you should bear in mind that – apart from the Practice Forum – they are all in Extended Services, which means that you are paying about 5p a minute for the time you spend there. If you spot some software that you fancy, just remember that running at 14,400 Baud, every 1Mb costs around £1 in on-line charges to download – more on a poor phone line.

9.9 Summary

- Newsgroups allow people from all over the world to share common interests and problems.

- There are over 6,000 newsgroups, covering almost every aspect of human (and alien!) life.

- As a newsgroup subscriber, you will receive articles regularly – possibly too many. Some groups generate huge numbers of articles, consuming large quantities of disk space.

- If your main interest in the Internet is membership of newsgroups and access to e-mail, then the off-line mail and news service WinNet, run by the PC User Group, is probably the best provider for you.

- Netscape offers access to all newsgroups, and this can be a good way to sample groups that sound interesting.

- CompuServe members have access to its forums, as well as to newsgroups through the Internet links. Forums have messaging areas, libraries of files and on-line conferences.

10

FINDING FILES

—— 10.1 Aims of this chapter ——

The Internet must be the greatest source of files in the World – there are countless Gigabytes out there. The trick is finding the ones you want. Net magazines, Net articles in other magazines and newspapers, Web pages and newsgroup articles all sometimes contain URLs of files that may be useful to you, but if there are specific files that you want to find, you need a tool to search the Internet. Archie is that tool.

In this chapter we look at running searches in Archie, both through WSArchie and by e-mail. We will also see how to locate files in CompuServe's libraries.

SHOP LOCALLY

As a good Net user, you should aim to keep your Internet traffic to the minimum – it leaves more resources for everybody else. Before you start hunting through the Internet for a file, see if it is stored in your service provider's libraries. Most hold copies of Net tools and other popular software.

—————— 10.2 Archie ——————

Let's start by being clear about what archie does *not* do. It does not connect to the 1,000+ **ftp sites** (Section 11) and search through their directories. That would make searching very time-consuming and wasteful of Net resources. Instead, it searches through a database that contains the names, locations and brief descriptions of the files stored in the ftp sites. This database is updated regularly, and copies are stored on the 30 or so sites that act as **archie servers** (14.4).

You can query an archie server interactively, using suitable software such as WSArchie, or by e-mail. There are advantages in both approaches, but before you try either you need to know three basic archie commands.

find *pattern*

This produces a list of files that match the *pattern*, giving their filename, site and directory location. How the *pattern* is interpreted depends upon the type of search. Unless you specify otherwise, archie will search for those filenames that contain the partial name that you have given.

set search *type*

The main *type* options are

sub – the default, that finds files where the *pattern* is a substring of the name. For example, a sub search for

    uuencode

will find:

    uuencode-1.0.tar.gz   (a Unix compressed file)
    uuencode.README
    uuencode.com   (the software)

sub-case – a case-sensitive version of sub, forcing a match to the same combination of capitals and lower case letters.

exact – the fastest type of search, but must be given the full filename and extension.

You can also tell archie to try **exact first**, then fall back to a sub-string or regex search (see below).

regex – where the *pattern* is a regular expression as used in the Unix utility *ed*. This accepts wildcards, ranges of characters and alternative patterns. The most useful of these are probably ^ (carat) . (dot) and the .* combination.

^ only allows a match if the filename starts with the pattern. For example,

        ^pk

will find

        pkunzip.exe

        pkz204g.exe

but ignore files with 'pk' elsewhere in their names.

. (dot) stands for any one character. Combined with an asterisk as .* it can stand for any number of characters. (Note the subtle difference from DOS where * alone has the same meaning.) These are not needed at the start and end of patterns, as a regex string acts just like a sub-string there. Use them where the middle part of the name is unknown:

        psp.*zip

will find

        pspic54a.zip

        pspic54b.zip

        pspic54c.zip

        pspro200.zip

If you want to know more about these expressions, or any other aspect of archie, send e-mail to an **archie server** (14.4) with the word 'help' in the body of the message.

set   match_domain

This restricts the search to one or more given domains, rather than searching all the world's ftp sites. For example,

> set match_domain uk

checks only ftp sites in the UK, and performs the search far more quickly than if it had to check everywhere. It is always worth trying a restricted search when you are after popular files, as there are often a great many copies of these.

You can specify several domains, separated by colons. For example,

> set match_domain uk:fr:se:ge

This will search UK, French, Swedish and German sites.

Most archie servers can also handle pseudo-domains – single words to replace sets of domain identifiers. For example,

> set match_domain usa

is equivalent to:

> set   match_domain   edu:com:mil:gov:us

Similarly,

> set match_domain westeurope

will cover the EC and Scandinavia, and save a lot of typing.

Each archie server has its own set of pseudo-domains. To find out what they are, send it an e-mail with the message 'domains'.

Other   commands

Archie responds to a number of other commands that can be used for fine-tuning your operations, but they are not needed if all you want to do is find files quickly and with as little fuss as possible. If you are interested, send a 'help' message to any archie server.

10.3 WSArchie

WSArchie is a **Winsock client** (6.5) that provides a simple but effective Windows-based interface for archie. It comes ready configured with the addresses of a set of archie servers and needs no other configuration before use.

To run a query through WSArchie, start by entering the find pattern in the **Search for** slot, and select the search type. If you want to limit the range of the search, enter a Domain code or psuedo-domain in the **Domain** slot. If you haven't got your Winsock connection running, do it now, then click [Search] to start Archie off.

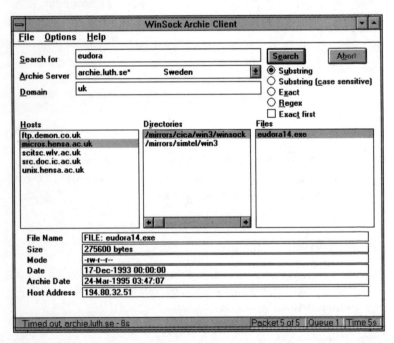

Figure 10.1 WSArchie after a successful search. When you are writing down the details of a file, note you may need to scroll the directory pane to get the full path.

Watch the status bar to find out what is happening. On the left it shows the archie server that you are connected to, and an estimate of how long it will be before it starts on your request. If this reads 900s, it is a pure guess, and could change dramatically in a few seconds. If you see a 'Timed Out' message when you first try to connect, there is a problem and you should [Abort] the search and try again, either there or at another site. If the 'Timed Out' message appears after the search has started, wait a moment to see if it clears itself, before aborting.

Over on the right it shows the number of requests in the **Queue**, ahead of yours and the estimated **Time** it will take to process your request. If you are faced with a long queue, abort the request and try another server. If the estimated processing time is more than 10 or 15 seconds, abort the request and limit the domains.

You know the search is running well when you start to see the **Packets** count building up. When this is complete, there is a delay of a few seconds before the details are filled into the Host, Directories and Files panes. Selecting a file from here brings fuller details of it into the slots at the bottom of the window.

If you want to download the file immediately, use the *File – Retrieve* command. This will run **WS FTP** (11.4) and transfer a copy on to your hard disk. If your search was for future use, make a note of the details of the file at the site nearest to you.

After you have been using WSArchie for a while, you may want to change the default settings for the server and type of search. To do this, use *Options – User Preferences* to open this panel. Note that you do not need to set your User ID.

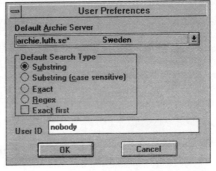

- 165 -

—————— 10.4 Archie by mail ——————

If you have tried using WSArchie, you may have noticed that it can sometimes take a while to perform a search successfully. You will sometimes have to try several different servers before you find one that will let you in; when you get there, you may have to join a lengthy queue; and when it does get round to your request, it does not always go smoothly. A lost connection in the middle of a search will put you back to square one. Don't let's get too gloomy – this is a worst case scenario. There are other days when you connect instantly, and your request is processed successfully in a matter of seconds.

Archie by e-mail pushes the problems off on to the archie server. You send off your request, get on with something useful and dial up your service an hour or so later to collect the results.

The message can be sent to any archie server. There are two in the UK, at Imperial College London (archie.doc.ic.ac.uk) and at Lancaster University (archie.hensa.ac.uk), but I find that I get the best service from one in Sweden (archie.luth.se). Whichever you use, you must put archie@ before the server's name:

    archie@archie.luth.se

No Subject line is needed – if you include one it will simply be taken as the first line of the message. The message is a simple list of commands. It could consist of a single line:

    find uudecode

which will do a world-wide sub-string search for 'uuencode'.

If you know a file's exact name, set the search type to exact for a more efficient operation; if it is a popular file, restrict the domain. Both of these options must be set before the *find* command. Your message might then read:

    set search exact
    set match_domain uk
    find uudecode.com

That request produces the following reply. At the top of the message you will see the commands and the resulting Search and Domain settings. The information you get about each file is the same as that from a **dir** (11.2) command in ftp.

This exact, restricted search produced only a small number of files – a compact example was wanted. Other searches will find far more files, and it is with these that the e-mail approach is perhaps more useful as it gives you a list that you can study at leisure.

```
>> set search exact
>> set match_domain uk
>> find uudecode.com
# Search type: exact, Domain: uk.
Host unix.hensa.ac.uk     (129.12.43.16)
Last updated 04:36 30 Mar 1995
    Location: /pub/matlab/contrib/tools
    FILE   -r--r--r--   2142 bytes  01:00 13 May 1994  uudecode.com

Host ftp.demon.co.uk     (158.152.1.44)
Last updated 06:01 24 Mar 1995
    Location: /simtel20/msdos/starter
    FILE   -rw-rw-r--   1158 bytes  02:00 12 Mar 1991  uudecode.com

Host micros.hensa.ac.uk     (194.80.32.51)
Last updated 05:47 24 Mar 1995
    Location: /mirrors/simtel/msdos/starter
    FILE    -rw-r-----   1158 bytes  02:00 12 Mar 1991  uudecode.com
```

Figure 10.2 An e-mail reply from an archie server. This gives all the information needed to download the file, and a bit more. The numbers after the Host names are their IP (Internet Protocol) addresses. There was a time when you had to use these to contact remote computers – fortunately that it no longer the case.

—— 10.5 Files from CompuServe ——

If you are a CompuServe member, you still have ftp access to the Internet. Their facility works in much the same way as WS_FTP, with a set of predefined sites and a panel to set up a connection to a specific site and directory. *Go ftp* will get you into this service – but be prepared for delays in getting through as it seems to be very heavily used.

You can also use the File Finder to locate and retrieve files from the extensive libraries in the **Forums** (9.8).

File Finder

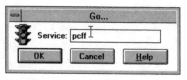

If you have a PC, use *Go pcff* to jump straight to the Finder for PC files. There are also finders for Macintosh, Amiga and Atari computers, and ones devoted to graphics and games. To get to any of these, use *Go filefinder*, and select from the list.

When you first reach File Finder take a few moments to read *About* the facility.

When you want to do a more complex type of search than the one illustrated here, there are a set of *Instructions* to guide you.

When you know what you want to do, select *Access File Finder*.

Note: The Featured Files are those described in the current issue of the Members magazine. You don't need File Finder for these, as their locations are given in the magazine.

The **Search Criteria** panel
offers a number of different
ways to perform a search.
With no criteria set, all the
files – 150,000+ at the time
of writing – are selected. You
can set one or more criteria
to reduce this to a manage-
able size.

Keyword searches are good
for exploring. You can set up
to three keywords – and
there is no special vocabu-
lary to learn here, just use words
which describe what you want. For
example, if you were looking for a
program to convert graphics between different formats, you might
try 'graphics' and 'utility'. After this
has been run, the Current selection
will be reduced to around 200 – still
rather a lot to hunt through!

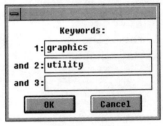

If you know what the file is called, then the simplest approach
is to search by File Name. The exact name is helpful, but not
necessary, as you can use of the * wildcard.

Suppose that you wanted to find a specific graphics conversion
program, such as Paint Shop Pro. It's a fair bet that its file
name starts with PSP but it might have a version number in
the name, and it may be stored as a ZIP or as an EXE file.
Telling it to search for PSP* will find any file that starts with
PSP no matter what follows these letters.

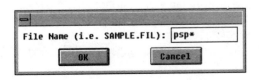

Once you have reduced the selection as far as you can, take the *Display Selected Titles* option. This brings up a list with the title, location and name of the files. There may not actually be as many as it seems, as some of the more popular software has duplicate entries in different libraries. Scroll through to find your file, then select it. This takes you to a panel with a full description.

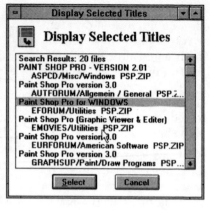

If, after checking the information and the size, you want to download the file, click [Retrieve] and set the filename and directory at the following dialog box.

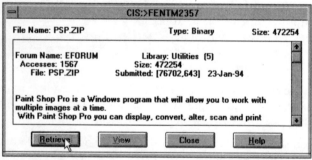

SHAREWARE AND FREEWARE

Many of the files that can be downlaoded from the Internet are freeware – no charge, no strings attached – others are shareware. Try these for free, but if you are going to make regular use of them, do register and pay the small fee. It helps to keep up the flow of good quality, cheap software.

10.6 Summary

- If you want to find a file that is stored somewhere on the Internet, you need Archie.

- The only essential archie command is find, but set search and set match_domain can improve the efficiency of your searches.

- WSArchie is a Winsock client that simplifies the process of running archie requests.

- Archie searches can be organised by mail, and this can sometimes be the most time-efficient way of doing them.

- CompuServe, like most service providers, has its own libraries of files. These can be browsed, but if you are looking for a specific file, the File Finder facility will help you to track it down.

11

FILE TRANSFER

11.1 Aims of this chapter

Once you have located a file, downloading is not difficult. You may well find that the hardest part about collecting files off the Internet is making the economic decisions about which ones are worth the phone time to download and the disk space to store them in.

The most efficient way to get files off the Internet is to use ftp, and that is the focus of this chapter; but it is not the only way, and we will also be looking at retrieving files from Web pages.

UPLOADING

If you have files – programs, pictures or text – that you think might be of interest to others, you can upload them on to the Net. But don't just stick them anywhere. Look for directories called 'uploads', or something similar, and check existing files to see if yours is the same kind of thing.

11.2 ftp

The ftp File Transfer Protocol is the standard way of copying files across the Internet. Exactly how that protocol works need not concern us – all we need to know is that it does work if we run ftp software on our machines and connect to a remote computer that is running the host version of ftp.

There is a small set of ftp commands that you may not need to use directly if you have a Windows ftp program. However, take a few moments to look at them, as they show what goes on during an ftp session. The examples given below work through the steps that will get a copy of PkZip – the shareware compress/uncompress utility. (Correct at the time of writing, but things change rapidly on the Net.)

open

The first task is to create a link to the remote computer and log in to it. We make the link with open followed by the name of the site:

        open   ftp.ibmpcug.co.uk

It normally takes a few moments to make the connection – but if the site is very busy, you won't get through. If all goes well, you will get a welcome message and the host will ask for your login name and then your password. When ftp'ing your user name is always '*anonymous*', and the password is your e-mail address.

        login: anonymous

        password: <your@e-mail_address>

chdir

You will then be linked to the remote computer so that it acts almost as another drive on your own computer. Initially, you will be at root level. You will almost certainly want to switch into another directory. To do this, use *chdir* (or *cd*) – it works the same as the MS-DOS command.

    cd   /pub/WinNET

You should then see the message *'250 CWD command success-ful'* – 250 is the code for the message.

dir

If you are exploring, rather than going after a known file, use *dir* to see what is in a directory. If the listing does not look the same as those you are used to from your PC, it is probably because it is coming from a Unix computer.

```
total  1980
-rw-r--r--  1 11 guest      104   Sep  9 02:34   compress.txt
-rw-r--r--  1 11 guest    27642   Sep  9 02:35   compress.zip
-rw-r-----  1 0  guest   667080   Aug 19 21:17   dmspring.exe
-rw-r-----  1 0  guest     2337   Aug 19 21:20   dmspring.txt
-rw-r--r--  1 0  guest   202574   May 27 20:45   pk204g.exe
-rw-r--r--  1 0  guest      741   May 27 20:47   pkreadme.doc
-rw-r--r--  1 0  guest    87745   Jul  6 21:41   unz51x.exe
```

Three things are important here.

The **name** is on the far right. You will need to note this
   carefully if you want to download the file;
the **file size** is in the middle – and having seen the size and
   worked out the transfer time you may decide *not* to
   download;
the **access permissions** are on the far left. There are three
   classes of user – the owner of the file, the other members
   of the same group, and everybody else. Different levels of
   access can be set for each. 'r' stands for 'read', which is
   what you need for copying, and your permissions are from
   the middle set. In sum, as long as the 5th character is 'r',
   you can copy.

binary and ascii

Files can be transferred in ASCII or binary mode. If you are transferring text, using ASCII mode will speed it up slightly; all other files must be transferred in binary mode. The commands to set the modes are simply:

    binary

or

    ascii

get

This does the copying. At its simplest, the command line is:

    get pk204g.exe   {or whatever filename}

This copies the file into the current directory on your system, retaining the original name. This is the easiest way to use it – files can easily be moved within your system later, if necessary.

quit

Use this to close down the connection.

─────────── 11.3 ftp URLs ───────────

We looked at these earlier, along with other **Uniform Resource Locators** (2.8), but let's look again and see how they work. Here, for example, is a URL that finds WS_FTP, a Windows ftp program:

ftp://ftp.halycon.com/local/seasigi/slip/windows/.suite/ws_ftp.exe

The **ftp:** at the start identifies it as a file that can be retrieved with ftp. The next item, **ftp.halycon.com**, is the name of the host computer. Many, though not all, ftp sites have names that start with ftp. The bulk of the URL, from the name, right the way through to the last slash, gives the path to the directory. In this case it is **/local/seasigi/slip/windows/.suite**. The very last item, **ws_ftp.exe**, is the name of the file.

To retrieve this file, the sequence would be:

```
open   ftp.halycon.com
anonymous                    {at the login: prompt}
<your@e-mail_address>        {at the password:}
cd   /local/seasigi/slip/windows/.suite
get  ws_ftp.exe
quit
```

—————————11.4 WS_FTP———————

This Winsock ftp software makes light work of file transfer, providing an easy interface to the operations. Setting up **WS FTP** (6.8) was covered earlier when we looked at **SLIP and Winsock** (6.2). Let's see now how it can be used to retrieving files from a remote computer.

The first step is to make your SLIP connection through Winsock, then get WS_FTP running. Next, click on the `Connect` button at the bottom right of its window. This opens a pane in which you specify the details for the connection. What is needed here depends upon several factors

1 If you have a considerate service provider, they will have pre-configured the software with the details of a number of sites. To use one of these, simply select one from the **Profile name** list, then go to step 3.
2 If no site information is stored, or you want to link to a different site, click on `New`, type a memorable name for the Profile; and the site into the **Host name** slot.
3 Click the **Anonymous login** checkbox to pull your e-mail address into the **Password** slot.

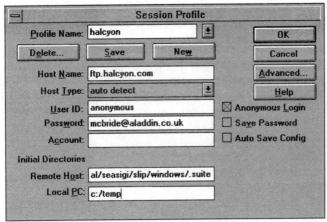

Figure 11.1 Setting up a new connection in WS_FTP.

4 If you know which directory you want to be in, type its path into the **Remote Host** slot.

5 If you want incoming files to be stored in a particular directory, type its path into the **Local PC** slot.

6 If you want to retain the details for a later trip to the same site, click [_Save_].

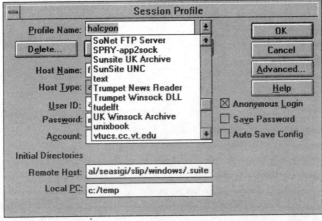

Figure 11.2 Selecting a site from the Profile list – you may still have to change the Remote Host directory setting.

7 Click [OK] to close down the pane and start to make the connection.

If you keep an eye on the little Log Window at the bottom of the WS_FTP window, you can watch the progress as it tries to link to the remote computer. All being well, the welcome message should scroll by, followed by another message as it changes to the required directory. There will usually by a delay while the directory listing comes in – and if it contains a lot of files, this can take a minute or more!

Many directories will have an INDEX or a README file. If you see one of these, take a few moments to read it. Select the file and click on [View] to pull it into your editor for reading.

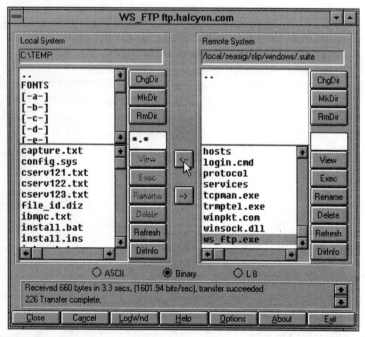

Figure 11.3 The connection has been made, we have reached the right directory, and have just selected a file for downloading.

If you want a closer look at the directory listing, or would like to retain a copy for future reference, click ▣ DirInfo . This will run Notepad and display the dir list in full. If required, it can then be saved from there, using the normal *File – Save* command.

When you find what you want to download, select it and click ▣ <- . A panel opens to show you how the downloading is going.

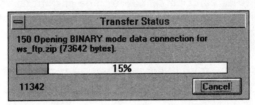

Note that if you decide to cancel the transfer, you are likely to confuse the system. Sort it out by clicking ▣ Cancel on the main WS_FTP Window.

When you have finished at the site, click ▣ Close to shut down the connection. This leaves the software running, so if you want to, you can reopen the Connect panel to link to another site.

THE THOUGHTFUL FTP USER

ftp sites normally have a limit on the number of anonymous users that can log in at any one time – they are almost all universities or commercial sites with in-house users, who must get priority. The more popular sites can get very crowded at times. Try to use them after the normal working day – remembering the US is 6 to 10 hours behind the UK – and try not to add to the congestion. When you are going after a specific file, if you do not have its URL, use **Archie** (10.2) to track it down. Aim to go straight in to the directory, get the file, and come straight out again. If you are just exploring, get the directory lists and study them off-line.

11.5 CompuServe ftp

If you are a CompuServe member, you still have ftp access to the Internet. Their facility works in much the same way as WS_FTP, with a set of predefined sites and a panel to set up a connection to a specific site and directory. *Go ftp* will get you into this service – but be prepared to be patient. It can take 20 or 30 seconds to open the first panel, and almost as long to move to the next step. Connecting to remote sites and into their directories always takes a while, whichever service you use.

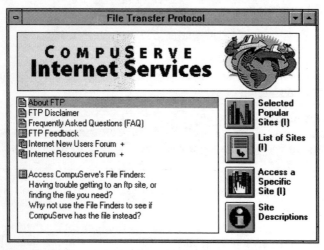

Figure 11.4 The top level ftp panel. You may find it useful to read About ftp when you first visit, and the Frequently Asked Questions are – as usual – the first place to check when you have a problem.

If you are just exploring, take the *Selected Popular Sites* route and try one or more of those. If, efficient and thoughtful ftp user that you are, you know what you want and where it is, use the *Access a Specific Site* option. This opens a dialog box in which you can type the name of the host and the initial directory path. The path is not essential, but it is a slow job changing from one directory to another, so leaping in at the right place is

Figure 11.5 Accessing a specific site through CompuServe ftp. Double check your typing before starting it off, as mistakes waste time. In this example we are off to Lancaster University, (micros.hensa.ac.uk) to get a file from their /mirrors/ cica/win3/util directory.

always a good idea. The User Name (anonymous) and Password will have been entered for you, so after checking that the site and path are written correctly, just click OK.

It can take a little while to make a connection, and the system might appear to have hung as nothing seems to be happening. However, be patient, and you should eventually see the welcome message from the remote host. Scan through it to see if there is anything of importance that you should note, then click OK to close it up.

There will be another delay while the directory list comes in and is sorted out before being displayed.

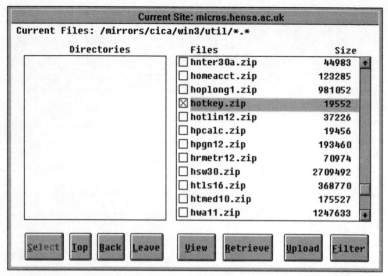

Figure 11.6 A directory listing from CompuServe's ftp facility. Note that clicking on a filename highlights it, but does not select it for transfer. You must check the box by the name to select a file.

If the directory listing is very long and you would like to focus in on part of it, click Filter and set the file specification as you would for a DIR command in MS-DOS; e.g. 'H*.ZIP' will select those ZIP files starting with H.

When you have located the file you want, click on the check box beside its name to select it, then click Retrieve. You will be prompted for a name and directory path for the file, and the transfer will then start.

The panel that shows the progress of the transfer can be quite useful – if nothing else, you can tell if you have time to make a cuppa while you are waiting.

———— 11.6 Files from the Web ————

As you browse your way around the Web, you will quite often come across ftp URLs for files. If they are hot-linked, then clicking on them should connect you to the site and to the file. If you have a Helper Application configured for that type of file, the application will be started and the file loaded into it. It can then be saved from within the application in the usual way. With an unknown type of file, Netscape will ask you what you want to do with it.

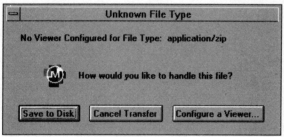

One of these options is ⟦Save to Disk⟧. Choose this, and a Save dialog box opens for you to set the filename and directory. Once you have OK'd that, the file will download into your system.

Yahoo's ftp sites

Chance encounters with ftp opportunities are all very well – and you really can find some good things that way – but you can also use your Web browser for regular ftps.

Go to **Yahoo** (www.yahoo.com), select **Computers** then **Internet** and you will find the option **ftp sites**. At the time of writing, this had 10 entries. Most of these were to specific sites, including the excellent ftp.luth.se – a wonderful source of files – but there is also the ftp Interface. This has links to all ftp sites. The complete list is horrendously long, but there are sublists, each holding sites from a section of the alphabet.

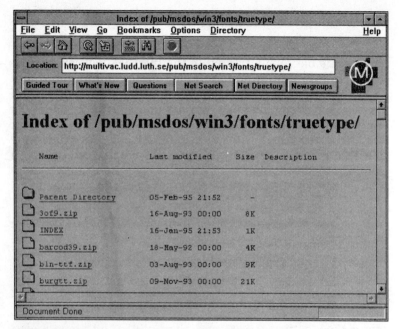

Figure 11.7 Using Netscape to connect to ftp.luth.se. At this stage, I have moved down through 5 levels of directories by clicking on their names. Clicking on a filename will get the Unknown File Type message, with the option to Save to Disk.

The site listings are light on information, with just a few indicating the types of files that they specialise in. However, they are all hot-linked, so if you have a URL and know where you are going, you can easily get from the list to the site. You will generally come into a new site at the top level of the publicly accessible directory and will have to work your way through the directory structure, one level at a time, to get to where you want to be. The directory listings can be saved if required, with the normal *File – Save* command. Once you reach your target directory and locate the file, it can be downloaded by clicking on it.

Netscape's ftp is not as direct as WS_FTP, but it works.

———————— 11.7 ftp by mail ————————

If you only have e-mail access to the Internet, you can get files by ftp, though it takes a little longer – sometimes a lot longer! A few sites run ftpmail server programs to handle e-mailed requests. They will connect to your designated site, change to the right directory, get the file and stick it in the mail back to you. If it is a binary file, it will arrive in ASCII form – and in several pieces if it is a large file – so you will have to convert it back into binary. But that and the delay between mailing the request and getting the reply, are small prices to pay for the facility.

Probably the best known ftpmail site is run by the DEC corporation (free of charge) at gatekeeper.dec.com. There is another at Princeton University and WinNet also handles requests.

In essence an ftpmail request is simply a list of commands. The main thing is that your typing must be 100% accurate. If you make a mistake, you will not know about it until your failed request is returned to you the next day!

As an example, let's look at a request that will retrieve the AtoB software from the hensa site. AtoB converts ASCII files back into binary, and is well worth having if you are going to use ftpmail, as the ftpmail server will use the equivalent BtoA to convert them into ASCII. The URL for this software is:

ftp://micros.hensa.ac.uk/mirrors/simtel/msdos/fileutil/atob11.zip

The request is addressed to:

ftpmail@gatekeeper.dec.com

The Subject line can contain anything. You might put:

requesting a copy of atob

The body of the message will read:

```
open   micros.hensa.ac.uk   anonymous   <your@e-mail_address>
 cd  /mirrors/simtel/msdos/fileutil
 get  atob11.zip
 quit
```

You should receive three items of mail in response. The first will be an acknowledgement of your mail; the second will be the requested file or directory listing; the third a log of the transactions with the remote computer. If the request goes wrong, you may be able to see why by studying this log.

—————— 11.8 Summary ——————

● ftp File Transfer Protocol is the standard means of copying files across the Internet. There are around 1,000 host computers that allow net users to download their files by ftp.

● ftp URLs can be recognised by ftp:// at the start. The site name is the item up to the first /; the file name the item after the last /; in between is the directory path.

● The Winsock program WS_FTP offers probably the most convenient way to run an ftp transfer.

● CompuServe has an ftp facility, but also has its own libraries of files.

● Thoughtful ftp users aim to locate a file first through archie, rather than browse directories, as this reduces their time on-line to sites.

● Files can be downloaded through Netscape, and ftp sites can be located through Yahoo by selecting Computers, then Internet.

● You can perform ftp by mail, by sending a request to an ftp server.

12

GOPHERSPACE

12.1 Aims of this chapter

The Gopher system was the forerunner of the World Wide Web, providing for the first time a unified system for accessing the wealth of information on the Internet. Its menu-based approach is neither as attractive nor as flexible as hypertext links, and in the last two years it has been overtaken in popularity by the Web. However, do not ignore it. There are times when Gopher offers the simplest way to track down information.

In this chapter we will use **HGopher** (6.9) to work through some menus and search for items. In the process, we will look at two key aspects of this software – setting up Viewers for different types of files, and creating Bookmarks, so that when you find useful sites you can get back to them easily in future.

GOPHER BY MAIL

You can run Gopher requests by e-mail! It is slow, but it works. See '*Access The Internet by E-Mail*'. Get a copy from:

ftp://mailbase.ac.uk/pub/lists/lis-iis/files/e-access-inet.txt

---

12.2   Gophering

If you can select an item from a menu, you can use the Gopher system – after a fashion. There is a bit more to it if you want to use it efficiently. Let's start by looking closer at a Gopher menu.

The item name is, of course, the most important thing. Not only does this tell you what it is, double-clicking anywhere on the name selects the item.

Immediately to the right of each heading is an icon which tells you the nature of the item. The ones you meet most often are:

link to another menu

link back to the previous menu

text file, to be read through Notepad or other editor

image file in gif, jpeg, bmp or other format

binary file – normally a program

sound file

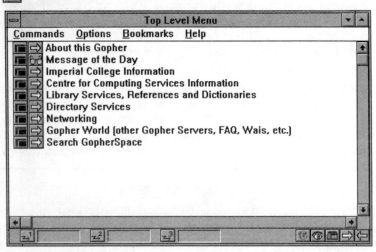

Figure 12.1 The top level menu at Imperial College (gopher.ic.ac.uk) – a good place to start from. Gopher World takes you to the top of a major menu system.

Menu items can, of course, be handled directly by HGopher, but most other types of items require additional **viewers** (12.3) – programs that can display, play or otherwise make sense of the file. Some may have been set up during installation; others you will have to add yourself.

If you click on these icons, you will see an *Info* label appear – sometimes accompanied by an *Admin* label. Drag the pointer over on to *Info* and when you release the mouse button a box will open showing the specification of the item. You can use these details when creating **Bookmarks** (12.4).

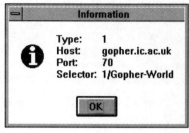

To the far right of some items you will see 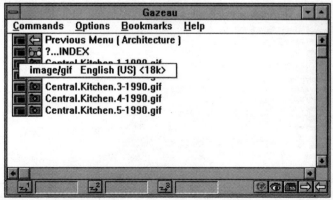. This indicates that alternative views of that item are available. Hold down the mouse button on this to find out about the nature and size of the file. If there are alternative views of the item, you can select one at this point.

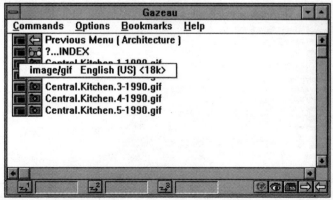

Figure 12.2 Holding the mouse button down on the leftmost icon makes a brief details panel appear. This menu contains images, with an index and the usual link back to the previous menu. If you want to know what a Gazeau 'kitchen' looks like, turn to page 191.

12.3 Setting up viewers

These perform the same function as **Helper Applications** (8.7)
in Netscape, extending the range of file types that can be viewed
while on-line. It is worth checking that you have viewers for
the more popular file types – bmp, gif and jpeg images, plain
and Word-formatted text – at an early stage. Others can be
added as needed later. Having a viewer ready configured is not
essential. Files of unrecognised types can be saved to disk for
viewing off-line.

Setting up is simple, as long as you have suitable software.

1 Use the *Options – Viewer Set up* command to open the
   Viewers dialog panel.
2 Pick a type from the *Select View Type* list.
3 Type the program name, with its path if necessary, into
   the *Viewer* slot.

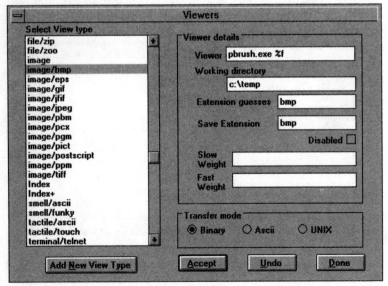

Figure 12.3 Setting up Paintbrush as the viewer for BitMap files.

4 Set a *Working Directory* if desired – your normal temporary directory will be used if this is left blank.

5 Give the *Extension*(s) that will identify files of this type.

6 Ignore the Weights slots – they are for advanced users!

7 Click [Accept] to record the details.

If you want to view the images that you will find as you work through the Gopher menus, you really need software capable of handling plenty of types. Either Paint Shop Pro, or Graphics Workshop will do the job, and both are shareware, available over the Internet. The image to the right is one of the Gazeau 'kitchens', a GIF graphic, captured here through Paint Shop Pro.

Be patient when viewing. Files download at around 20k a minute over a 19,200 Baud link.

——— 12.4 Bookmarks ———

As Gopherspace is so huge, you will sometimes have to work through up to a dozen or more menu selections to get to a particular point. The Gazeau kitchen, for example, was reached through the sequence:

```
gopher.ic.ac.uk (Imperial College top level)
    Gopher World
        Gophers by Subject (a good place to start any research)
            Fine Art
                Image Art
                    Kodak CR Rom
                        Architecture
                            Gazeau
```

As it takes a few seconds to download each level of menu, you don't want to have to go through this sort of sequence more often than necessary – nor do you have to. You can set up your own menus of *Bookmarks*, giving direct links to any items in the Gopher system.

If, while you are using Gopher, you come across a menu or an item you want to keep for the future, open the *Bookmarks* menu and use either *Mark Menu* or *Mark Item*. At the end of the session you must use Bookmarks – Save to store the current set of Bookmarks on disk.

If you find the listed details or the URL of an interesting item you can add this to your Bookmarks set while you are off-line.

1 Run HGopher, without Winsock.
2 Use *Bookmarks – Load* to open an existing set. You should have DEFAULT.GBM, if you have not saved any yourself.
3 Give the *Bookmarks – Create* command to open a dialog box, and enter the details.
   Type is normally Menu, pick from the list if not;
   Description is what you want in your Bookmark menu;
   Host is the site name;
   Port is normally 70, unless it clearly states otherwise;
   Selector is the path – include any slashes.

Where the details are given in full, copying them into the dialog box is simple, as each part should be identified. For example:

Figure 12.4 Creating a Bookmark in HGopher. If you are not told the Port number, it will be 70.

```
Name=Internet  Wiretap  (Music)
Type=1
Path=/Library/Music/
Host=wiretap.spies.com
Port=70
```

Where you have a URL, you will have to extract the details:

```
gopher://wiretap.spies.com:70/Library/Music
```

Where the Port is the standard 70, it is regularly omitted from URLs. If the connection is to the top level menu of a site, there will be no path. A URL could be as simple as this one – it takes you to the University of Minnesota, the home of Gopher:

```
gopher://gopher.micro.umn.edu/
```

——— 12.5 Search engines ———

There are two main tools for searching Gopherspace – *Jughead* (Jonzy's Universal Gopher Hierarchy Excavation And Display) and *Veronica* (Very Easy Rodent-Oriented Net-wide Index of Computerized Archives). The two are similar, though Veronica is more sophisticated and can be more productive. Both look for one or more given words in the titles of menu items, and produce a menu of matching items. Try to be specific – broad searches can find hundreds of links.

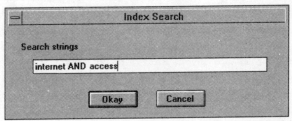

Figure 12.5 Setting up a search, using Jughead, for items on access to the Internet. A veronica search could start the same way, though the AND is optional there.

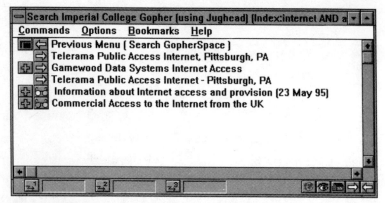

Figure 12.6 The result of a Jughead search for *Internet* and *Access*. The same search through Veronica produced five times as many items, but took far longer to run – one of the problems is finding a Veronica server that is open for business and not overcrowded already!

Jughead and Veronica can both be found on Yahoo's Computers – Internet menu, giving easy access to Gopherspace from the World Wide Web.

12.6 Summary

- Gopher menus can contain links to other menus and text, graphic and audio files.

- You will have to configure viewers to be able to display some types of files on screen while you are gophering.

- If you start from the Gopher World menu, you can reach all places in Gopherspace, but you may have to work through many layers of menus to get there.

- By storing the details of sites and menus as Bookmarks, you can easily return to useful places.

- A Jughead or Veronica search will find menu items that relate to a given subject.

13

USING HTML

13.1 Aims of this chapter

Many service providers now offer free or cheap Web pages to their personal customers, and many companies are realising that a presence on the Web is almost essential if they want to be seen as modern, international businesses. If you are not thinking about setting up a Web page at the moment, you could well be doing so soon. Do not be daunted by the prospect. HTML – HyperText Markup Language, nicknamed HoT MetaL – is not difficult to use. You can soon learn enough to knock up a respectable Web page, with graphics and links to other files and pages.

This chapter introduces the tags that are used to style and lay-out the text, and shows how you can include graphics and create links to other Web pages.

If you want to go further, there are a number of books around on using HTML, and it is very easy to discover how others have achieved their effects. If you save a Web page as a file, while you are in Netscape, you can open that file in a word-processor and see its HTML tags and references.

—— 13.2 Tags and references ——

In HTML, all styling is done with tags. These are mainly in pairs, one at each end of whatever is being styled. They are easily recognised and follow simple rules:

- a tag is always enclosed in <angle brackets>
- the opening and closing tags of each pair are identical except for a / before the identifier in the end tag
- tags can be written in either capitals or lower case
- tags can be on the same line as the enclosed text, or on separate lines – it makes no difference to the layout.

For example, to get a second level heading – 18 point bold type – the tags are <h2> and </h2>. These two sets of lines:

```
<h2>This is a sub-head</h2>

<H2>

This is a sub-head

</H2>
```

Both produce this same effect:

This is a sub-head

Use whichever form is easiest to read in your text file.

The file can be created in any word-processor or editor that can output plain ASCII text – Write does the job nicely. Save the file with an .HTM extension – this is not essential, but it does help to identify it as a Hypertext file.

Commonly used tags

```
<HTML>.....</HTML>
```

Mark the start and end of the HTML file.

<HEAD> .... </HEAD>

Mark the header area, that will hold the title. The remainder of the text is the body and is enclosed by:

<BODY> .....</BODY>

<TITLE> ..... </TITLE>

Whatever is marked as the title is displayed in the window's title bar, and used as an identifier by the **Bookmark** (8.6) system in Netscape, and by some other Internet utilities.

<H1> .... </H1>

This is the first level of heading, typically producing 24 point bold type. You can have up to 6 levels, tagged <h2>, etc, each producing progressively smaller bold type. The actual effect of any header can be defined within some Web browsers.

<B> .... </B>

These format the enclosed text in bold. If you want to emphasise with italics, use:

<I> .... </I>

As well as these tag pairs, there are a few single tags that are used to control layout

<HR>

Draws a Horizontal Rule (line) across the screen.

<P>

Marks the end of a paragraph, and causes a single line gap before the next item. If the tag is written on a separate line it will make your text file clearer to read.

Forces a break on to a new line, but without creating a space between paragraphs. Typically used in simple lists of items, or in multi-line addresses.

<ADDRESS> ..... </ADDRESS>

Use these tags to enclose your e-mail address, which is normally placed as the last item on the page.

13.3 Graphics

Though Netscape and other Web browsers can handle a variety
of graphic file formats – if they have had helper applications
configured – their 'native' formats are JPEG (marked by JPG
or JPE extensions) and GIF (CompuServe's standard). Use these
if you can, rather than the PCX or BMP files that are produced
by Paintbrush. They will ensure that anyone who browses to
your page will be able to see the pictures. The GIF format has
good compression – typically producing files of less than half
the size of the same image saved as a PCX. JPGs tend to be
larger as they use a 16 million colour format.

To include a graphic in your page, use the tag img src, followed
by the filename.

<IMG   SRC="wincim.jpg">

The key point to note here is that you must give the path to the
directory if the file is in another directory to the html file.

<IMG   SRC="images\mylogo.gif">

13.4 Hotlinks

I have left these until last in this quick tour of HTML, but
hotlinks are really the most important aspect of hypertext. There
are three types of links, but they all derive from the same basic
Anchor, using an <A> tag with a reference to the linked item.

<A HREF=reference> Hotlink text </A>

This puts the standard hotlink format – normally coloured and underlined – on the text, as well as creating the link.

To link to another file, the *reference* is the filename, with a path if necessary.

```
<A HREF="compserv.htm"> ..... </A>
```

To link to another Web page, or any other file on the Internet, the reference is its **URL** (2.8). For Web pages, this means that the reference will start "http://...

```
<A HREF="http://www.yahoo.com"> .....</A>
```

To link to another part of the same document, you must first set up an anchor at the point that you want to jump to. The target anchor simply sets up an identifying name.

```
<A NAME="page2"> </A>
```

The hotlink to the named point follows the normal pattern – but note the # in front of the name.

```
<A HREF="#page2">Go to page 2</A>
```

You can combine the references to create a hotlink that jumps to a named point in a file.

```
<A HREF="compserv.htm#forums"> CompuServe Forums </A>
```

This would link to a point taggled with <A NAME="forums"> in the compserv.htm file.

HOTLINKS TO HTML

If you want to find out more about using HTML, point your browser to the HTML Primer:

http://www.ncsa.uiuc.edu/General/Internet/WWW/HTMLPrimer.html

And for more details and pointers to HTML software, head for *Yahoo* and from the main index select *Computers*, then *World Wide Web* and finally *HTML*.

——— 13.5 Writing a Web page ———

Before you start to write html, take a few moments to compare
some Web pages with their files. Next time you are on the Web,
find some interesting pages – ones with graphics, hotlinks to
other parts of the document and to distant pages, and save them
to file. (They will have .HTM extensions.) Close down the connection, restart Netscape if necessary, and reload one of the
pages, using the *Open File* command. Open the same file in
Write, and set the windows so that you can look at them at the
same time.

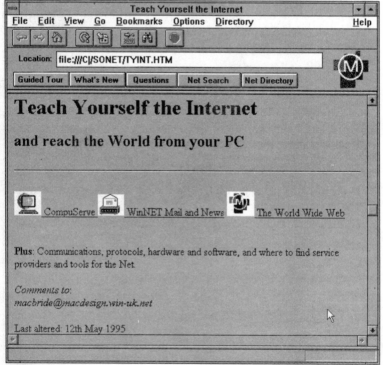

Figure 13.1 A simple html document, seen here through Netscape using the
Open File command.

```
<HTML>
<HEAD>
<TITLE>
Teach Yourself the Internet
</TITLE>
</HEAD>
<BODY>
<H1>Teach Yourself the Internet </H1>
<H2>and reach the World from your PC</H2>
<HR>
<P><IMG    SRC="wincim.jpg">
<A HREF="compserv.htm">   CompuServe </A>
<IMG     SRC="docs/winnet.jpg"><A     HREF="http://www.win-
uk.net">   WinNET Mail and News</A>
<IMG   SRC="winwww.jpg"><A   HREF="http://www.yahoo.com">
The  World  Wide  Web</A>
<P>
<B>Plus</B>: Communications, protocols, hardware and soft-
ware, and where to find service providers and tools for the Net.
<P>
<I>Comments  to</I>:  <ADDRESS>macbride@macdesign.win-
uk.net</ADDRESS>
<P>
Last altered: 12th May 1995
</BODY>
</HTML>
```

Figure 13.2 The text file that produced the page shown opposite.

To test out effects, you can edit the text file, save it and then reload it into Netscape. It is probably the best way to understand the way that different tags work.

———— 13.6 Summary ————

- An HTML document is a simple text file with tags to set styles and anchors to create hotlinks.

- Tags are normally used in pairs, turning effects on and off. Some, such as those that mark the ends of paragrahs and draw lines between items, are used singly.

- Graphics can be included in HTML pages by writing references to them in the text.

- You can create hotlinks to other Web pages, to files elsewhere in your directory structure, and to other parts of the same document.

- One of the best ways to see how to create effects in HTML is to compare the text version of the document with its display in Netscape.

- Many service providers now offer the opportunity of setting up your own Home page on their systems.

14

SITES, SOURCES AND SERVERS

——— 14.1 Service providers ———

There is no lack of organisations offering access to the Internet. At the last count there were over 1500 worldwide, with all but the smallest countries having at least two or three alternatives. Listed below are a very small selection of these providers in the UK, the US and around the world. They are not necessarily the best value – and what pricing/usage structure is best value for you depends upon how much you use the Internet. However, all can provide (reasonably) local access throughout their respective countries, and should serve as your first provider. Once you are on-line, and can judge your needs more accurately, you will find links to access providers worldwide at Yahoo. Go to:

     www.yahoo.com

and work through the menus Computers and Internet – Internet – Internet Access Providers – Regional – Countries.

● Some providers run an e-mail and news only service, usually in addition to full Internet access.

● Many organisations also offer conferencing, file libraries, on-line multi-player games and other services to their members.

● Costs may well have changed – generally downwards.

UK

The BBC Networking Club
Cost: £25 registration, £12 p.m.
E-mail: info@bbcnc.org.uk   Tel: 0181 576 7799

CompuServe See page 207
Cost: £6.50 p.m. plus on-line charges for extended services
E-mail: 70006.101@compuserve.com   Tel: 0800 289 458

Delphi Internet
Cost: £10 p.m. for 4 hrs then £4p.h./£20 p.m. for 20 hrs then £1.80p.h.
E-mail: ukservice@delphi.com   Tel: 0171-757-7080

Demon
Cost: £12.50 registration, £10 p.m.
E-mail: sales@demon.net   Tel: 0181 371 1000

EUNet GB
Cost: £95 per quarter
E-mail: sales@Britain.EU.net   Tel: 01227 266466

GreenNet
Cost: £5 p.m. + £3.60 p.h. peak, £2.40 p.h. off-peak
E-mail: support@gn.apc.org   Tel: 0171 713-1941

PC User Group (CONNECT)
Full Internet access
Cost: £14 p.m. (WinNET Users £7.25 p.m.)
E-mail: info@ibmpcug.co.uk   Tel: 0181 863 1191

PC User Group (WinNET) See page 208
E-mail and news only
Cost: £3.25 per hour, minimum £6.75 per month
E-mail: request@win-uk.net   Tel: 0181 863 1191
Dialup: 0181 863 6646 login as 'winnet'

Pipex
Cost: From £180 p.a.
E-mail: sales@pipex.net   Tel: 01223 250120

US

NetCom
Cost: $17.50 p.m. unlimited off-peak, 40 hours peak time
E-mail: sales@netcom.com

Thor Net
Cost: $10 p.m. for 40 hours
E-mail: sales@thor.net

WinNET Communications
Cost: $19.95 p.m. for 4 hours, then $5.40 p.h.
(Nationwide access through freephone 800 lines)
E-mail: info@win.net

Australia

OzEmail
Cost: $2.50 p.h. nights, $5 p.h. daytime
Tel: 02 391 0480
E-mail: sales@ozemail.com.au

Internet Access Australia
Cost: $40 p.m. for 60 hours
E-mail: accounts@iaccess.com.au

Hong Kong

Asia-Online
Cost: $120 setup, $120 p.m. for 20 hours, then £2.95 p.h.
E-mail: info@asiaonline.net

Ireland

Ireland On-Line
Cost: not available over the Net
Tel: 335-1-8551739
E-mail: sales@iol.ie

Israel

NetVision
Cost: $50 p.m. for 40 hours
Tel: -1-972-4-8550330
E-mail: sales@netvision.net.il

New Zealand

ICONZ (Internet Company of New Zealand)
Cost: restructuring at time of writing
Tel: 495-2960
E-mail: webmaster@central.co.nz

Singapore

Pacific Internet
Cost: $9.95 p.m. for 10 hours, then $2.95 p.h.
Tel: 1-800-872-1455
E-mail: info@pacificnet.sg

South Africa

Internet Africa
Cost: R960 p.m. unlimited
E-mail: webmaster@iafrica.com

—— 14.2 Introductory Offers ——

CompuServe

CompuServe is the longest-established and largest of the on-line information services, with over 3 million members. It offers access to **e-mail** (Section 7), **newsgroups** (9.2), **ftp** file transfer (11.5), and the **Web** (8.11) as well as running many services for its members.

If you want to dial in and register, use these settings:

Phone number: 0171 490 8881
Communications: 7-E-1 = 7 Data bits, Even Parity, 1 Stop bit
Baud rate: anything up to 9600

When you dial in, at each *prompt* give the **response** as shown:

CONNECT:	press **[Enter]**
Host name:	**CIS** (CompuServe Information Service)
User ID:	**177000,5606** Note the comma!
Password:	**EXPLORE/WORLD**
Agreement number:	**TEACHYOURSELF**
Serial number:	**93006**

When you get on-line you will be asked to register – have your credit card details at hand. The introductory offer gives you a month's free usage of the basic services, plus £10 credit for the extended and premium services. You can keep a track of your usage by checking your account in the Member Services area.

CompuServe supplies CompuServe Information Manager, in Windows, DOS and Macintosh formats. You can ask for this to be sent to you by post, or download it. If you want it straight away, see **Binary Transfers** (5.7) for details.

If you pefer you can phone (Freephone 0800 289378) for your free membership kit including WinCIM 1.4 and NetLauncher diskettes. Specify which version of the software you need and quote ' Teach Yourself the Internet'.

—— **14.3 ftp sites and sources** ——

ftp.demon.co.uk – good source of Windows and DOS utilities. Start at the /pub/ibmpc directory

ftp.uwp.edu – major games site, and often too busy to get into! Start at /pub/msdos/games

ftp.microsoft.com – Microsoft's own. Good source of upgrades, add-ons, bug-fixes, hints and tips.

micros.hensa.ac.uk – carries mirrors (copy) of the cica and simtel sites, major sources of software. Start at /mirrors.

sunsite.unc.edu – major ftp site sponsored by Sun Computers.

src.doc.ic.ac.uk – (Sunsite UK) lots of material, but a busy site.

software.watson.ibm.com – IBM's software database.

ftp.ibmpcug.co.uk – (PC User Group) specialising as the UK movie database server.

Internet tools by ftp

PKZip – ftp.univie.ac.at/system/dos/fileutil/pkz204g.exe

WinZip – micros.hensa.ac.uk/mirrors.cica/win3/util/winzip55.exe

uuencode / decode – micros.hensa.ac.uk/mirrors/simtel/msdos/ starter/uuencode.com and uudecode.com

WinNet Mail – ftp.ibmpcug.co.uk/pub/WinNET/wn_news.zip

Trumpet Winsock – sunsite.doc.ic.ac.uk/computing/systems/ ibmpc/simtel/win3/twsk20b.zip

Netscape – ftp.ed.ac.uk/pub/WWW/pc/clients/netscape/ns16-100.exe

WS_FTP – dorm.rutgers.edu/pub/msdos/winsock/apps/ws_ftp.zip

HGopher – ftp.kfunigraz.ac.at/pub/communication/dos/ hgopher24.zip

Eudora – ftp.qualcomm.com/windows/eudora/1.4/eudora144.exe

Paint Shop Pro – ftp.luth.se/pub/msdos/win3/desktop/pspro200.zip

Text files

'**Hitchhiker's Guide to the Internet**' by Ed Krol –
bells.cs.ucl.ac.uk/rfc/rfc1118.txt

'**There's Gold in them thar Networks**' by Jerry Martin –
bells.cs.ucl.ac.uk/rfc/rfc1402.txt

—— 14.4 Archie servers ——

United Kingdom
archie.doc.ic.ac.uk   archie.hensa.ac.uk

Europe
archie.edvz.uni-linz.ac.at   archie.funet.fi
archie.luth.se   archie.rediris.es
archie.switch.ch   archie.th-darmstadt.de
archie.univie.ac.at   archie.unipi.it
archie.uninett.no   archie.univ-rennes1.fr

North America
archie.ans.net   archie.internic.net
archie.cs.mcgill.ca   archie.rutgers.edu
archie.sura.net   archie.uqam.ca
archie.unl.edu

—— 14.5 Gopher servers ——

gopher.aston.ac.uk (Aston)   gopher.bham.ac.uk (Birmingham)
gopher.cam.ac.uk (Cambridge)   gopher.ed.ac.uk (Edinburgh)
gopher.liv.ac.uk (Liverpool)   gopher.ic.ac.uk (London)
gopher.newcastle.ac.uk   gopher.nottingham.ac.uk
gopher.wlv.ac.uk (Wolverhampton)

INDEX